Studies in the History of Law and Justice

Volume 26

The purpose of this book series is to publish high quality volumes on the history of law and justice. Legal history can be a deeply provocative and influential field, as illustrated by the growth of the European universities and the *Ius Commune* , the French Revolution, the American Revolution, and indeed all the great movements for national liberation through law. The study of history gives scholars and reformers the models and courage to question entrenched injustices, by demonstrating the contingency of law and other social arrangements. Yet legal history today finds itself diminished in the universities and legal academy. Too often scholarship betrays no knowledge of what went before, or why legal institutions took the shape that they did.This series seeks to remedy that deficiency.

Studies in the History of Law and Justice will be theoretical and reflective. Volumes will address the history of law and justice from a critical and comparative viewpoint. The studies in this series will be strong bold narratives of the development of law and justice. Some will be suitable for a very broad readership.

Contributions to this series will come from scholars on every continent and in every legal system. Volumes will promote international comparisons and dialogue. The purpose will be to provide the next generation of lawyers with the models and narratives needed to understand and improve the law and justice of their own era. The series includes monographs focusing on a specific topic, as well as collections of articles covering a theme or collections of article by one author.

Gianfrancesco Zanetti

Equality and Vulnerability in the Context of Italian Political Philosophy

Italian Efficacy

Springer

Gianfrancesco Zanetti
Department of Law
University of Modena and Reggio Emilia
Modena, Italy

ISSN 2198-9842 ISSN 2198-9850 (electronic)
Studies in the History of Law and Justice
ISBN 978-3-031-35552-3 ISBN 978-3-031-35553-0 (eBook)
https://doi.org/10.1007/978-3-031-35553-0

This Springer imprint is published by the registered company Springer Nature Switzerland AG
The registered company address is: Gewerbestrasse 11, 6330 Cham, Switzerland

Contents

Chapter 1
Introduction: Teaching Under Unusal Circumstances

An old science-fiction story by Frederick Pohl, "The Gold at the Starbow's End," starts out with a fictional experiment. Some children are in a room cluttered with stuff, and they are told to reach another room down the corridor, as fast as they can, without touching the floor with their feet—a task they manage to carry to completion by tying to their feet some long wooden boards they find in the room, and then sliding their way to their assigned destination. In a second phase of the experiment, only one board is left in the room: the children promptly tie the very same rope to one end of that wooden board and hop lightly while pulling the rope. This latter device significantly improves their performance: they succeed in reaching the second room in a shorter time. The problem, the obstacle, was the second board. Too much of a good thing, as they say.[1]

When I was appointed to the Chair of Italian Studies at the University of California, Berkeley, I found myself in a similar predicament. I had to plan my Ph. D. classes in the middle of the health emergency brought on by the COVID-19 pandemic, and that meant, apart from other quite unhelpful circumstances, no access to any library. I had to rely on my own tiny personal library at home, and on my memory (and, well, the Internet). For some reason, however, I felt less clever than Pohl's fictional children. It was challenging and somewhat distressing. The subject I had agreed to lecture on was "Equality and Vulnerability in the Context of Italian Political Philosophy".

Since it was of course mandatory to teach *online*, but it was almost verboten to do so *remotely*—that is, from outside the mainland US—I had to happily hop a flight to San Francisco.

Because of a quarantine, and of the other COVID-19 restrictions, I would spend most of my time in the city secluded in a comfortable basement (my personal library had shrunk to a suitcase) reading over and again (and then again) some famous pages

[1]" Pohl (1972). See also the extended version: Pohl (1982).

G. Zanetti, *Equality and Vulnerability in the Context of Italian Political Philosophy*, Studies in the History of Law and Justice 26,
https://doi.org/10.1007/978-3-031-35553-0_1

written by Cardano and Machiavelli, poetry by Campanella and by Vico, legal musings by Santi Romano and Arturo Carlo Jemolo. The lack of time constraints made it possible to settle into an unusual frame of mind for my studying routine.

My students, on the other hand, were exceptionally gifted and supportive. I could never quite understand how they could follow my classes in such an easy, almost relaxed way (despite all the inconvenience of the pandemic environment, and despite my *cute* Italian accent, as one student described it). Their questions were challenging and focused. We had the time to go back to the original text any time we felt the need, or the whim, to do so. They could evidently read both Italian and Latin. One of the students was Brenda Rosado, who like me was a Townsend fellow.[2] Our chair was the indefatigable Timothy Hampton, and every Tuesday it was one fellow's turn to discuss a paper chosen (and posted online) by one in our number, on a subject that most of the time, most of us were completely unfamiliar with (it fell to me to comment on a remarkable paper by Bob Sharf on a Buddhist sect's notion of time: it did prove to be a busy week, that one). It was more than interesting to be exposed to so many different stimuli, to get the benefit of engagement with a group of fellows intellectually so diverse, to converse with colleagues who did not share my outlook and were not privy to my academic jargon, to face a gentle and yet challenging and sharp audience. And it was, of course, fun.

The confluence of such unusual circumstances was perhaps responsible for my idiosyncratic approach to the subject of the course. Thus Hans Kelsen, the father of modern Continental jurisprudence,[3] is mentioned mostly as a Dante scholar; Gerolamo Cardano comes up as a favorite author of Marcello Dell'Utri, a political ally of (former libertine Italian prime minister) Silvio Berlusconi who served time in prison because of his alleged connections with the Sicilian mafia, Cosa Nostra; the work of Giuseppe Mazzini is discussed, among other reasons, because of the bold parallel he drew between three vulnerable groups: women, black slaves in the American South, and republican Italians.

The idea, in working these angles and pursuing these tangential trains of thought, was to see if in some key texts in the tradition of Italian political philosophy there could be detected a realistic notion of *efficacy*, and this was the first problem I had in mind. The subtext all through the course—and the second problem addressed in prodding and canvassing these key texts—was that of equality and vulnerability, the idea here being to see if this problem could be tackled without invoking a specific notion of, say, natural law: to this end it was enough to rely on a bare notion of efficacy, and one that was not even deliberately articulated with any special theoretical awareness.

To make a long story short, on a notion of efficacy of this kind, normative horizons within which legal and political decisions can, and do, flourish are self-originating phenomena (a notion I introduce by a cursory reading of a lesser-known author like Nevizzano). These phenomena nevertheless offer their own legitimizing

[2] Doreen (2020–21).

[3] The Austrian legal philosopher and jurist, incidentally, taught at UC Berkeley. See Losano (2008).

narrative. Such a narrative, to this end, must present itself in a certain guise, as grounded in universal values, for example, or as a having a theoretical and genetic *prius* with respect to the phenomena themselves. Efficacy phenomena, however, do not really need to function according to the narrative they historically radiate; on the other hand, it is almost impossible to conceptualize these phenomena except through that very narrative (or through some other narrative), that is, except by endorsing or criticizing, validating or debunking that specific narrative.

Efficacy is the notion I use in canvassing Machiavelli's texts, where these problems can first be somehow detected. When Gerolamo Cardano tries to find a name for this special factor, he actually calls it, very much *en passant*, efficacy, *efficacia* (*quae maximum est*).[4]

Such efficacy is not going to create nicely shaped systems endowed with unity: we actually have only efficacy *phenomena*, more or less arbitrarily subsumed under a system by a narrative that radiates from the phenomena themselves. The narrative is precisely what allows the observer to perceive them as such, that is, as efficacy phenomena, coexisting with a narrative, no matter how crude, that is not just a noetic condition for understanding them but is also an alethic condition for their existence. The narrative, on the other hand, exists *because* of them, and has no status or function other than that of making those phenomena intelligible and existing *as efficacy phenomena.*

This respect for efficacy phenomena gives to some Italian authors a specific (and well-known) flavor of hard realism, a pragmatic *gusto*, which is even stronger when it does not sound theoretically deliberate or intentionally provocative—and therein, of course, and quite often, lies part of their charm.

Most of these authors were directly engaged in contemporary politics: they held office and were often responsible for making legal, political, or military decisions. They had to struggle and fight: some of them (Machiavelli, Lottini, Campanella) were physically tortured; others (Dante, Mazzini) spent part of their lives in exile; one (Pasolini) ended up being killed; Cardano and Braibanti served time in prison. Only few of them, like the Marquis Beccaria or Vico, were lucky enough to have had sources of distress that, for the most part, were only private (Beccaria had issues with his father, Vico with his son); Santi Romano, after a stellar professional life, happened to die before his old age could be disturbed by the political and legal consequences of his allegiance to Mussolini and Fascism. This is a peculiar gang of fellows, and I picked them mostly because I find them intriguing, and because I thought my Berkeley students would enjoy reading them. Apparently, they did.[5]

Needless to say, the idea is not that Italian authors deliberately carry on a special tradition, but rather that specific themes run through different texts, resurfacing here

[4]Cardano (1630), Caput LVIII. See footnote 82.

[5]With the exceptions of *New Science* by Vico and *Proxeneta* by Cardano, we mainly focussed on relatively *short texts*. It was, however, unfortunate that I had to neglect Paruta, Lottini, Campanella, and many others. Skipping Gianfrancesco Lottini was particularly painful.

and there, while different motivating factors urge the different authors to touch those theoretical points.

There is a resemblance with these scholars' intertextuality. Most of them were avid readers of Latin authors, and they sometimes mention them and sometimes just quote them taking for granted that their readers can recognize the sources. So, for example, to read Matteo Palmieri without being acquainted with Cicero and Sallust is almost to read a different author. The point, nevertheless, is that there is not *a* Latin philosophical doctrinal tradition that is upheld by these scholars: there are themes, catchwords, famous passages which it feels good to quote, and which seem to support a *specific mode of critical thought*, and there is also a way of dealing with some concrete contemporary problems.

There is therefore no Italian political-philosophical agenda, nor, certainly, is there any shared awareness of such a specific thread: but the thread *is* there, and though it takes the form of a patchwork of afterthoughts and hints dropped in the margins, it is nevertheless interesting (at least I hope it is), and it sheds some indirect light on a few intriguing corners of this tradition. One of such dark corner is the notion of equality as a practice.

1.1 Equalities

In the chapter on Vico, the only one previously published as a freestanding paper,[6] a distinction is drawn between two kinds of equality. The notion according to which human beings are equal in some fundamental and compelling sense (basic equality) is distinguished from equality as a policy aim (normative equality). There can be little doubt that we need a notion of basic equality to advance our egalitarian aims, and that while much has been written about equality, modern literature deals far less with the background idea that humans are, fundamentally, one another's equals.[7] This is, of course, the grand scheme to be found, for instance, in Thomas Jefferson's Declaration of Independence: "We hold these truths to be self-evident, that all men are created equal, that they are endowed by their Creator with certain unalienable Rights, that among these are Life, Liberty and the pursuit of Happiness." Equality first, then, and it is a basic equality—human beings *are* (created) equal: unalienable rights will imply some kind of normative equality.

The problem is that, as I would argue, notions of basic equality can be conceived as cultural constructions (albeit of the most valuable kind): they can be the outcome of normative equality practices.

If, for example, I believe in the basic equality of all human beings, I will likely be ready to fight for the civil rights of subjugated minorities, just as Giambattista Vico's *famuli* (plebeians) seem ready to fight for their equal rights while realizing that the

[6] Zanetti (2011), pp. 461–470.

[7] Waldron (2002), pp. 2–7.

patricians "did not come from heaven," after all. But that is not yet a complete description of Vico's philosophy of equality. The *famuli* fought, first and foremost, because, as it happens, they must have grown weary (*se ne dovettero attediare*) of being oppressed and subjugated.[8] At the end of the day, no special philosophical argument was required. They wanted equality, period. *In* fighting and *by* fighting they *became* equal, because they changed the normative horizon within which both they and the patricians dwelled.

In other words, the idea is that some kind of inequality and discrimination is eventually perceived as such, and that these painful circumstances trigger a practice of normative equality that in turn will create a new set of shared beliefs, a new world of meanings, and a new (more inclusive) kind of basic equality. This perceived injustice does not need to be exhaustively deduced, as such, from any set of moral absolutes, from any metaphysically grounded anthropology, from any notion of natural law; and, conversely, the practice does not need to be justified in absolute theoretical terms. This is the residual legacy of the background notion of efficacy: it shows itself in self-originating phenomena. Needless to say, equality practices will themselves secrete some kind of narrative, some (normative) arguments for equality.

This path from equality practices to basic equality does not seem intuitively consistent with a religiously inspired tradition of natural law. While it *is* intuitive that, if we are all children of the same God, we probably enjoy some kind of basic equality, the counterintuitive idea of a basic equality that is not *found*, but rather *forged*, achieved, obtained, or seized, feels puzzling and somehow troubling. Indeed, the first time we were urged to *reach* equality (rather than *acknowledge* it), to create some equality where there is none, the plea came from the Serpent itself: *Eritis sicut Deus, scientes bonum ac malem*,[9] the words beloved by Goethe's Mephistopheles,[10] and it did not end up well.

This means that it is possible to conceptualize basic equality as an effect, a *posterius*, a result, an outcome, a point of arrival, while a practice of normative

---

[8]Vico [1744] (1990) edited by Andrea Battistini (Mondadori), p. 696. See also Vico [1744] (1999) in the English translation by David Marsh (Penguin).

[9]Gen 3:5. For God knows that in the day you eat of it your eyes will be opened, and you will be like God, knowing good and evil.

[10]Wofgang Goethe, *Faust*, Act I, Scene IV. "This Serpent's adage round your memory twine,/ You'll one day fear your human face divine": *Goethe's Faust* [1808] (1843) translated by George Lefevre, M.D. (Charles Jugel) p. 78. The wise words that advise *not* to get involved in an equality practice are those addressed by Abdiel to Satan in Milton (*Paradise Lost* VI, 174–181):

Unjustly thou deprav'st it with the name
Of servitude to serve whom God ordains,
Or Nature; God and Nature bids the same,
When he who rules is worthiest, and excels
Them whom he governs. This is servitude
To serve the unwise, or him who hath rebelled
Against his worthier, as thine now serve thee,
Thyself not free, but to thyself enthralled.

equality can be deemed as the starting point, the input, the cause, the *prius*, the necessary pragmatic assumption. This, of course, means that we need to ask what can be the motivating factors of normative equality practices—the "reasons" for such practices.

It should be noted that there is no logical contradiction between the two alternative conceptual paths, from basic equality to equality as an aim, and from equality as an aim to basic equality; Vico was well aware of the former path. Even so, the very possibility of the counterintuitive path from equality as a goal to basic equality, next to the traditional path moving in the opposite direction, dramatically alters the overall argumentative meaning of the standard (liberal) notion of equality. Unfortunately, domination and oppression can and do *make* groups of humans basically *unequal*, as both Vico and Giuseppe Mazzini found out. This is specifically cruel, like trying to breed human beings destined to submission and oppression.

Inequalities, in the plural, are often hidden in plain sight, just like the purloined letter imagined by Poe.[11] Yes, Vico's *famuli* fight for universal equality: that is achieved only when full citizenship rights are granted to everybody within the boundaries of the Empire. The only fly in the ointment is that, well, women—roughly half the population—are left out. It is not so much that the answer to the question "Which men (i.e., which males) deserve to be citizens, to be 'equal'?" can change. It is that the relevant question itself can change when one can step outside the circle of those shared beliefs that crystallize within a given institutional and normative horizon.

Most famously, those inequalities that are the outcome of a given (contingent) institutional horizon usually conceptualize themselves as eminently natural: *aliquid monstri aliter*, mumbles the patrician who suspects that his pregnant wife had lain with a slave;[12] growing in that womb is a chimera, a monster with two different natures. The republican Italian "apostle," Giuseppe Mazzini, would bitterly mention that old biased argument: Italians are not apt, not ready, for political autonomy and freedom.

1.2 Vulnerability

Inequalities come in a variety of flavors. Equalities, in the plural, are those political and legal practices, not necessarily peaceful, that challenge a given and perceived inequality. From this point of view there is no (capital E) Equality—a perfect state of affairs, a "value" that can be fully grasped and described; there are only equality *practices*. While Equality must each time claim to be universal, it can never achieve that status. Especially aware of this open texture of equality practices is Mazzini, who particularly stresses this point.

[11] Poe (1844), ed. Van Doren Stern (1945), pp. 439–462.

[12] Publius Terentius Afer, *Andria*, 250, quoted by Vico (1990); cp. pp. 688, 740. 743.

All that we are left with are therefore *situated* equalities. There is no such thing as universal equality: there are only practices of normative equality that, in different circumstances, once different kinds of inequality and discrimination have been detected, reshape the notion of basic equality implied by different norms, institutions, and practices. A different normative horizon, one that conceptualizes itself as more inclusive, then emerges from within those norms, institutions, and practices.

Equality is a therapy—actually, a diverse condominium of therapies—for quite different kinds of diseases: it is not a state of good health. Equality is an *aequalitas aequans*, never an *aequalitas aequata*. Against every normative equality practice there can be levied the charge of having forgotten about those who in one way or another are left out, and there is always somebody who is left out. There is always a specifically relevant issue, a situated, hot-button problem—sometimes smoldering in silence, sometimes burning and blasting.

The very possibility of challenging a given allocation of wealth or status, a contingent normative horizon, is quite meaningful. From this point of view, any legal and political order comes with those limits built into the possibility of such a challenge. Such limits are not conceived as "boundaries": they rather dwell in those interstitial gaps that lie in the overlap of different narratives. Jemolo would speak of "islands" that the law can only lap but never submerge, islands like the family, an institution that for the Catholic lawyer was supported by different and powerful narratives that were alternative to the legal narrative, and potentially incompatible with it (though *narrative* is a word that, *ca va sans dire*, Jemolo would never have used): family is thus a *kosmion* of primal instincts and of religion, incendiary stuff that can put up a good fight against the disciplinarian power of abstract legal systems.

This, however, is a critical point. Uncomfortable though this may make us feel, there is no need to conceive a normative horizon as a monad sealed out from competing and overlapping narratives. Legal systems are no exception. It is of course quite tempting to fashion normative horizons into nicely shaped, mutually exclusive entities. Normative phenomena, however, do not need to adapt to any intellectual or doctrinal comfort zone.

Even when a legal system conceives of itself as absolute, one could argue, its limits will lie not *around* it, like boundaries, but *within* it. Even the Enlightenment and enlightened thinker Cesare Beccaria eventually had to admit as much when he faced the normative reality of that special encompassing group of gentlemen who would feel duty-bound to break the law by entering into a duel to protect their honor—a notion at odds with some tenets of the legal system, but which nevertheless had to be housed within it. Nothing prevents *other* normative systems from dwelling within the same normative horizon. We do not have to conjure up the challenges of postmodern multicultural phenomena to shed light on the softly unsettling reality of normative pluralism. Such pluralism famously becomes one of the main tenets in the thought of Santi Romano, who more than a century ago, and even before embracing Fascism and Italian racism, challenged Kelsenian normativism and offered his bold, almost outrageous, version of a plural institutionalism.

Such a pluralism, if conceived as a constitutive, inescapable feature of legal and political systems, provides a useful background assumption for the notion at play of "equality practices": normative arguments, one could argue, will radiate from the minority, encompassing groups whose shared and alternative beliefs can challenge the mainstream narrative. Normative arguments can pierce through the bubble-like sphere of those shared beliefs that contingently can turn into an efficacy point, a point which narrates itself as a justified normative horizon, and which can discriminate and displace, hurt and intimidate: it can create and *make* some kind of (basic) "inequality," that is, a specific vulnerable group.

Discrimination, oppression, or displacement can take quite different forms: coming in handy at this stage of the discussion is the notion of vulnerable groups.

Rather than focusing on an essentialist notion of human vulnerability—something I am not ruling out in the least: that is actually a promising research avenue—it is here more interesting to lay emphasis on heterogeneous, contingent, "situated" forms of vulnerability. There is no need for any notion of human nature (no need to reject the possibility, or the potential usefulness, of such a notion, either).

Any institution implies some kind of potential exclusion, framing a specific inequality in the very normative horizon it identifies itself with: Dante's most powerful attempt to conjure up a universal institution—using up, in the process, all the power of the *principium unitatis*—ends up giving us a *world*: what it gives us, therefore, is rich with exclusions (but it must nonetheless claim it harbors none). As was previously mentioned, it is very rarely that these inequalities and exclusions can be clearly perceived as such, because they are embedded in the very horizon from which a critical argument should radiate (the work of Cesare Beccaria played a role in the obliteration of situated vulnerabilities, an obliteration which, it may be argued, lies at the core of Western liberal democracies). The process by which an equality argument arises out of a given normative horizon, questioning and challenging that inequality, is the same process by which a form of situated vulnerability starts to be perceived as such.

Situated vulnerabilities, however, are not like colors or musical notes: they do not have to share any common feature or logic. Situated vulnerabilities are bound up with the contingent scenarios that originate together with a dotlike bubble of normative efficacy, which is why their emergence cannot be easily predicted or their logic shared by those who, by choice or by lot, dwell within the "limits" of that given set of institutions—the perceivable side of the efficacy bubble, the graspable narrative radiating from that given normative horizon.

Italian *racism* was (and is) more multifaceted (and probably quite worse) than it looks at first sight: the one and the same Italian Jewish scholar (Lombroso) could elicit scorn from racists because of their racism and from others because they thought *he* was racist. The one and the same Italian author of children's books (Salgari) had no qualms about glamorizing what elsewhere would have been labeled as miscegenation—love between Caucasians and Asians—while indulging in some most racist remarks about other Asians. The one and the same Italian subgroup (the Etruscans) could be held up as a noble race that enriched the Italian bloodline, while also being dismissed as a temporary, and ultimately negligible, stain on the genetic makeup of the Italian Aryan race (and in fact both positions could be found in the same racist journal). Racism is a motivating factor that can give rise to cruel efficacy phenomena; such phenomena radiate arguments that should rationalize the motivating factor, but that do not need to be consistent with one another.

Finally, the perceived vulnerability of the institutions themselves, of the contingent scenario, is just a special case of situated vulnerability—one that can sometimes trigger the most extreme reactions. Exemplifying the severe, cruel interaction of different kinds of vulnerabilities is the dark tale of the infamous "Braibanti affair", where the overlapping, intersectional vulnerability implicit in membership in different outside-the-mainstream minorities violently clashed with the perceived fragility of the same normative horizon that needed to marginalize and displace such figures of vulnerability—and therefore needed to crush the life of Braibanti himself.

Equality arguments are therefore both an answer to and a symptom of a perceived situated vulnerability, if and when normative horizons are conceived as mere efficacy phenomena understood through the narrative they radiate. In the Italian tradition of political and legal philosophy there is this theme that occasionally crops up here and there without any clear line of development.

1.3 Equality as a Practice

The realist and pragmatic attitude of some of these authors is therefore linked to a perceived phenomenon of vulnerability, to the emotions this phenomenon entails, to the pain and weariness attendant on oppression of one kind or another—and this perception (which in itself is no rational argument) can take the form of an equality practice (which *can*, by contrast, be an argument).

This link developed in a rather simple way: there is nothing mysterious, nothing glamorous about it. The "realist" attitude of some Italian authors—for example, and most notably, the author of the *The Prince* himself, Machiavelli—implied an utmost respect for so-called technical rules, rules which state the appropriate kind of means to a given end, but which are unable to choose the end itself. Technical rules, however, exhibit a specific feature—they seem unable to fully explain efficacy phenomena without the aid of *other kinds* of rules, constitutive rules that crystallize shared beliefs of some kind into a set of institutions, like a civic religion or a patriotic army. Machiavelli obviously never dreamed of using terms such as *constitutive rule*, but the point is that while an army of citizen-soldiers is technically expedient, because other kinds of armies are quite dangerous, it is still true that also implicit in such an army are emotions, feelings, values, or fundamental choices that cannot fully be understood in terms of technical expediency (or of a rational maximizer's self-interested computations).

Some authors need to negotiate the fine line between the world of functional expediency, the realm of technical rules, and the world of institutions, where duties and obligations arise and dwell. This is just another way of saying that efficacy phenomena present themselves through the narrative they radiate: the power asymmetry implemented by way of technical rules cannot be fully thought if we bracket away the institutional *world* shaped by those shared beliefs.

Such institutions are themselves vulnerable, because they necessarily imply some kind of situated vulnerability of an encompassing group (or of some such groups) and can therefore be challenged by equality practices (which practices most likely conceive themselves as fully revolving around a substantive notion of equality).

Equality as a practice is no sport for *anime belle*: it is not the leisure activity of well-meaning soft souls, blissfully unaware of the tough rules of the political world; it is a way of making sense of that very world, at the same time criticizing those valuable narratives of universal equality that are meant to somehow legitimize bare efficacy phenomena.

On the other hand, the criticizing is often done by exposing what lies behind the legitimizing narratives: the bare cruelty of exclusions, the stark inequalities. It is a procedure that scrutinizes "the king's scepter" and[13]

> removes from it the laurel,
> And reveals to the people how much blood,
> How many tears yet drip from it [...].

There is a constant going back to some harsh, painful political reality, a disdain for utopian dreams, a down-to-earth attitude, and a cold realism. There is a sanguine acknowledgment of the power asymmetries behind normative horizons: and a red thread connects Vico's merciless description of a heroic aristocracy to Santi Romano's dry remark that institutions are not meant to necessarily embody any equality. One must resist the temptation to call it a *pars destruens*. It *would* be such, a *pars destruens*, if it could be set in contrast to a *pars construens*. But that is not the case: it is only about negotiating the fine line between the logic of efficacy phenomena and the kind of equality practice one feels motivated to instantiate.

One last, and most important, caveat. This red thread is certainly not the key to understanding Italian political thought. There are, I am sure, far more important aspects, critical problems, and fundamental questions. The idea was just to elaborate on a cluster of problems that seem to crop up here and there as we read some Italian authors—a reading exercise that could shed light on some corners of their trains of thoughts, leaving some vaster areas in the dark. This is just a way of allowing some of their texts to react to such a deliberately non-neutral reading. In other words, no (new) interpretation of Italian political thought is offered here: just some *Discorsi* on some problematic aspects in the thought of a few Italian authors.

They had not originally been thought as chapters of a book. I made no attempt to edit them and polish them—they are still the texts of my Berkeley classes, that I would post on line for my students after the Wednesday afternoon class. These "lectures" make use of different methodological approaches: for example, Dante is explored through a single reading of his work (by Hans Kelsen); Machiavelli is

[13] Foscolo [1807] (2015), pp. 156–158.; "Of the Graves" in "Rediscovering Foscolo: a Translation of the 'Sepolcri' and of three sonnets", translated by Valentina Bianchi.

mostly approached through a "mechanical" text analysis; *The Duties of Man* by Giuseppe Mazzini is read as a text almost independent from the historical contingencies that motivated its creation; and so on.

My biggest debt is with Thomas Casadei; his support was always generous, intelligent, and compassionate. Mariano Croce, Tommaso Greco, Antonio Merlino, Giorgio E.M. Scichilone, Elio Tavilla have all read and commented parts of this book. Their comments and wise advice were invaluable. Special thanks go to Rosaria Pirosa for reviewing the entire work with great care and expertise; and for helping me to deal with some thorny theoretical issues. I shall miss our conversations at the CRID (Research Center on Discriminations and Vulnerabilities, University of Modena and Reggio Emilia) in the summer of 2022.

I am grateful to Albert Russell Ascoli, Timothy Hampton, Brenda Rosado, Mortimer Sellers, Barbara Spackman, and Kendall Thomas for their encouragement and support. Mia Fuller, chair of the Department of Italian Studies, was a most gracious, generous, and intelligent host. The *rettore* of the University of Modena and Reggio Emilia, Carlo Adolfo Porro shielded me from many bureaucratic poisons that could have prevented me from enjoying my UC Berkeley adventure. The Berkeley students who attended my course were the *Menschen* every instructor would like to teach to and engage with—and to them are owed my final and most heartfelt thanks.

References

Cardano G (1630) Proxeneta, seu De Prudentia. Paulus Marceau, Genoa. Italian edition: Cardano G (2001) Il Prosseneta ovvero della prudenza politica (trans: Cigada P). Mondadori, Milan

Doreen B (2020–21) Townsend Center for the Humanities, Berkeley

Foscolo U [1807] (2015) Of the Graves. Trans. Bianchi V. In: Bianchi V, Rediscovering Foscolo: a Translation of the 'Sepolcri' and of three Sonnets. https://www.academia.edu/22334674/REDISCOVERING_FOSCOLO_A_TRANSLATION_OF_THE_SEPOLCRI_AND_OF_THREE_SONNETS. 2015

Goethe W [1808] Faust. English Edition: Goethe W (1843) Goethe's Faust (trans. Lefevre G, M.D.) Charles Juge, Frankfurt o.M

Losano MG (2008) Scritti autobiografici. Diabasis, Reggio Emilia

Poe E-A [1844] The Purloined Letter. Poe E A (1945) The Portable Poe. In: Van Doren Stern P (ed) Viking, New York, pp 439–462

Pohl F (1972) The gold at the Starbow's end. Condé Nast, New York

Pohl F (1982) Starburst. Ballantine New York

Publius Terentius Afer, Andria, 250, quoted by Vico G, [1744] Scienza Nuova. Italian edition: Vico G (1990) Opere (ed: Battistini A) Mondadori, Milan, pp 688, 740. 743

Vico G [1744] Scienza Nuova. Italian edition: Vico G (1990) Opere. In: Battistini A (ed) Mondadori, Milan

Vico G [1744] Scienza Nuova. English edition: Vico G (1999) The New Science (trans: Marsh D) Penguin, London

Waldron J (2002) God, locke, and equality. Christian foundations in locke's political thought. Cambridge University Press, Cambridge

Zanetti GF (2011) Vico on equality and marriage. Ratio Juris Int J Jurisprud Philos Law 24(4): 461–470

Chapter 2
Dante Alighieri, Hans Kelsen, and the *Principium Unitatis*

2.1 Kelsen on Dante

Dante is, of course, too large a subject for a single lecture, chapter, or even book. His works defy our current typologies. The *Comedia* itself is, yes, a work of poetry, but it is at the same time a work of philosophy and of politics, of theology and law. This is, again, not news to anyone. The *De rerum naturae* by Lucretius is first and foremost poetry, but it is at the same time one of the most important sources in order to understand the Epicurean philosophy. The *Summa Theologiae* by Aquinas is, well, mostly theology, and yet it is a key text for natural law scholars and others. It is certainly legitimate to label the works by Dante Alighieri sometimes as poetry and sometimes as political philosophy, but such labels are only a starting point, not the outcome of a deep scrutiny.[1]

I would like to focus on a given interpretation of Dante, the interpretation given by Hans Kelsen. Kelsen did teach at Berkeley (where he died in 1973).[2] He came to the United States when the shadow of Nazi politics was falling on Europe. His very life was in danger, because he was Jewish. As every law student knows, Kelsen was probably the most important philosopher of law, the most outstanding jurisprudence scholar, in Europe at that time. His works are, even now, a cornerstone and a landmark for the scholarly community. He is the key author used in order to understand Legal Positivism, the notion that law is something artificial, man-made. Something which is not found in the realm of nature or reason but created by a human authority.

According to Kelsen, legal systems were nothing else but pyramids of norms (although this trope of the pyramid, often and correctly associated with Kelsen, is not

[1] See Steinberg (2013).

[2] See at least Kelsen (1934); Kelsen (1992), translated by Bonnie Litschewski Paulson and Stanley L. Paulson (Clarendon Press Oxford).

G. Zanetti, *Equality and Vulnerability in the Context of Italian Political Philosophy*, Studies in the History of Law and Justice 26,
https://doi.org/10.1007/978-3-031-35553-0_2

directly mentioned in his works), and States were nothing but such legal systems. Natural law played no role in such a consistent, rigorous idea of legal system, and morality would dwell in a separate domain, because any content, never mind how twisted and unfair, could be "law".—*Daher kann jeder beliebige Inhalt Recht sein.*[3]

In Kelsen every norm has its origin in another norm. Rudolf Virchow (and before Virchow the great scientist and politician Francois Vincent Raspail) had suggested that *omnis cellula e cellula* (every cell comes from a cell).[4] There is a basic consistency and unity in living, organic entities. And there is some kind of purity as well, because such entities are made of cells, and by nothing else, and cells come from cells, and from nothing else. According to Kelsen, as it were, *omnis norma e norma*; the State, i.e., the legal system, is nothing but norms on different steps of a hierarchic pyramid. His theory is "pure" because it acknowledges this fact. It does not need to meddle with religion or morality, with politics or theology.

Italian scholars reacted to his "pure theory" with a sense of discomfort. They sometimes felt that it was too abstract. The first footnote of Santi Romano's masterpiece, *L'ordinamento giuridico*, was a critique of Kelsen.[5] Fascist scholars were outraged that the State, with a capital S, could be dissolved into a dry network of legal norms, laws and statutes and judicial decisions. On the other hand, after World War II, some other scholars attacked Kelsen's pure theory because at the end of the day it has nothing to offer against the threat of totalitarian regimes, which use law as an instrument of raw power.[6]

Kelsen, however, did not first appear in Italian scholarly journals because of his jurisprudence genius: but because of Dante. The *Italianisti* at that time were quick on the uptake, and they did not miss Kelsen's contributions to Dante's *Monarchia*,[7] Dante's *Staatslehre* (State Theory).[8] One could even state that Kelsen's *fortuna* in Italy starts and ends with Dante, because after 60 years the Bologna publisher Boni asked his permission to print again his book on Dante, a permission that Kelsen granted under condition that it would be clearly stated that it was just the same book printed again, and not a "second edition".

While Kelsen seems to perfectly master the whole *corpus* of Dante's works, he focuses primarily on *De Monarchia*. His book is structured in the old-fashioned way. First the historical background. Next Dante's general philosophy. Then state theory,

---

[3]Kelsen (1960), p. 201. In other words: "To be sure, the law is no longer presupposed as an eternal and absolute category; its content is recognized as subject to historical change, and the law itself, as positive law, is recognized as a phenomenon conditioned by temporal and spatial factors". Kelsen (1992), p. 21.

[4]Virchow was an amazing figure. See for instance Eisenberg (1986), pp. 243–250.

[5]Romano (2017), p. 1. See in this volume, *Social Pluralism, Efficacy & Equality. Rethinking The Legal Order by Santi Romano*, section 9.

[6]Capograssi (1952), pp. 767–810.

[7]Arrigo Solmi wrote a critical note with a nationalist flavor. See Solmi and Kelsen (1907), pp. 98–111.

[8]Kelsen (1905); Kelsen (2017), namely *Lo stato in Dante. Una teologia politica per l'impero*, with a Preface by Giuseppe Monateri and Afterword by Tommaso Edoardo Frosini (Mimesis).

and afterwards connections parallels and differences with contemporary authors and scholars. Vittorio Frosini genially wrote that with such a *Monographie* Kelsen could have become *Privatdozent*.[9]

2.2 The Power of the *Principium Unitatis*

It is crystal clear that a key notion in Kelsen's Dante is the *principium unitatis*, the principle of unity. Kelsen stresses that the notion of pluralism, of varieties of any kind that cannot be subsumed into some form of unity, are most repulsive to the Middle Ages mind.

This is perfectly shown in Dante's cosmic geography, where a static round earth is surrounded by the heavenly spheres of the planets and of the "fixed stars" of the Ptolemaic astronomy, by the *primum mobile* (an in-between spherical "sky", kind of an intermediary step between Creator and creation), and finally by the Empyrean—which is at the same time *outside* (so that the weight of the whole universe is pressuring and castigating Lucifer, blocked by his sin at the center of the earth) and *center* of the cosmos. There is an Aristotelian flavor in this hierarchy of movements that needs to end up in an "unmoved mover" or "prime mover", *primum movens*—The Empyrean Sky, God Almighty Himself.

Unity is consistent with hierarchy—even in the hierarchy of evil and pain, the inverse pyramid of the funnel-shaped hell described in the *Commedia*.[10] I would add that there is something reassuring in this geocentric order. The human mind can grasp this unity in an almost natural way, with the additional bonus that the whole universe seems to revolve around humanity, with a sprinkle of cosmic narcissism that flatters our vulnerability and weakness.

This unity principle takes many shapes. A famous one is the allegory of the *tunica inconsutilis*,[11] Christ's seamless coat that the soldiers could not cut. Interestingly, this allegoric figure is used by Pope Bonifacius VIII, Dante's archenemy, in the notorious *Unam Sanctam* (*One and Holy*), a document where the Pope claims for himself *plenitudo potestatis*, power above every creature including the King of France (who in that moment was more dangerous than any Emperor). The Church is One, just like the seamless coat that the soldiers took from Jesus before the Crucifixion. Since "the coat was without seams, woven from the top throughout", the soldiers could not "rend it", and they decided to "cast lots for it".[12] The head of the Church, in the hierarchical pyramid of the ecclesiastic institution, is the Pope. More than this, the Pope is on the top of every hierarchical pyramid of human

[9] See Cau (2004) and Lagi (2008), pp. 32–34.

[10] A complete translation of the *Commedia* is to be found, for example, in Musa (1995).

[11] Dante (1112–1113); Dante (2015) edited by Quaglioni, pp. 150, 440. I found the contribution by Quaglioni invaluable.

[12] John 19: 23–24.

institutions. He is, theoretically, above the kings and the Emperor, because his power comes directly from God.

Dante makes use of this very same image. The Empire is one, and it controls, or should control, all human beings living in all the territories of the Earth. Such an Empire is, in Dante's time, wildly utopian. There was no sign in Europe that nations and peoples, kings and princes, could somehow bend their knee in front of a common and shared *imperator omnium.* It does not matter. When Dante speaks of the state, says Kelsen, he always means the world state, the universal state.

There is here, again, more than an echo of "the Philosopher". The philosopher *par excellence* is of course Aristotle. There is, at the very beginning of Aristotle's *Politics*, the famous tale of the origins of the polis (the city-state). Men and women are attracted because of reproduction, while master and slave congregate because of "conservation" or survival issues. The overlapping of these relations gives birth to the first community, the household or family (*oikos*). Several families congregate because of those needs that a single family cannot take care of, and such is the origins of villages (*komai*). Villages too are not enough, so that they have to congregate to form a city-state, *polis*, which is perfect not because it is faultless but because it does not need to grow anymore. It is independent.[13] This is the origin tale of the *polis* by Aristotle, a tale "from the beginning" (*ex arches*). Dante uses this same scheme, adding two steps: cities need to be unified into kingdoms, and kingdoms finally under one Empire.

It is critical to understand that Aristotle's tale, *ex arches,* is not necessarily a wholly scientific description, the way we could say: first there is an egg, then a tadpole, and finally a frog. A frog can grow old but it does not need to turn into another being. If we see something that looks like a frog but that has never been first an egg and then a tadpole, that being is *not* a frog. It is something else, (a toy, a robot, whatever). Aristotle was perfectly aware that there were city-states (*poleis*) that did not have this kind of origin—the colonies. His origin tale has a normative meaning. We should reason about the *polis* as if this were its origin. In other words, this tale basically explains the most important features of the city-states from an Aristotelian point of view. For example, the almost biological process by which different communities blend together into more articulate and complex entities makes sure that in a given *polis* there are some shared values (religion, mores, etc.). While different cities go hunting for happiness in different ways,[14] and have therefore different ways of life, within a given city-state, there is not much room for minority lifestyles of any kind.

The tale of the origins of the Empire provided by Dante presents itself as an empirical account of the way the universal state should and will take shape. It is, however, an account that presents itself as definitely more nuanced than any empirical description. If we think of cities and kingdoms as naturally subject to a *monarchia* not identified with the Church, we create the ideological background we

[13] Aristotle, *Politics*, I: 2.

[14] Aristotle, *Pol.* VII: 8.

need in order to accordingly conceptualize State and Church. Kelsen, most famously, kindly rebukes Dante for not having been brave enough to claim for the Emperor the top position. When everything is ready to take this final step, when all the premises are clearly stated, at the very end of his treatise, in a short paragraph Dante hastily adds that Cesar should look up to Peter with a reverent attitude, the way the elder son looks at his father.[15] It is a pyramid with two tops, it is something unacceptable for Kelsen.

On the one hand Kelsen's Dante is to be understood only by acknowledging the role played by the *principium unitatis*. On the other, Dante is criticized by Kelsen because he does not dare to draw the consequences from such a principle. Caesar should be the one, single top of the pyramid.

2.3 Borders and Limits

The *principium unitatis* is quite active in Dante's consistent praise of monarchy as the best possible form of government. This too was a theme well known by Aristotle, and Aquinas.

First, it is worth remarking (and Kelsen does) that Dante often speaks of *genus humanum*. The whole of mankind is and should be subject to the power of the Emperor. The unity of mankind is somehow necessary, for Kelsen-Dante. It is a logical premise of the universal monarchy. This unity seems to assume the necessity of a universally shared Christian faith, a notion that would have stressed the key role of the Church, a thorny issue for Dante. The territory of the universal empire was all the earth, the *mundus*. Thanks to his geocentric astronomy, Dante could truly claim a strong notion of universality for the territory of his Monarch. The *globe* was the whole human universe. He could therefore speak about sections of the planet that neither he nor anybody else had ever personally visited. Hans Lindahl, however, distinguishes *globe* from *world*. Globe is the surface of a sphere, the imperfect sphere of planet earth. A global law has no borders. It is an inside with no outside. World, however, is an intersection of meanings, an overlapping of human understandings lit up from within. A world must have some *limits*, because it necessarily excludes something. The opposition is no longer domestic versus foreign, but known versus *strange*.[16]

---

[15] Dante (1312–1313); Dante (1996), edited by Prue Shaw (Cambridge University Press), p. 94: "Let Caesar therefore show that reverence toward Peter which a firstborn son should show his father, so that, illumined by the light of paternal grace, he may the more effectively light up the world, over which he has been placed by Him alone who is ruler over all things spiritual and temporal".

[16] Lindahl (2018), pp. 28, 35. Lindahl elaborates on Bernhard Waldenfels's phenomenology of the alien (*Phänomenologie des Fremden*). See Waldenfels (2011) and, previously, the original publication: Waldenfels (2006).

It is crystal clear that the power wielded by Dante's Emperor is without borders. He has legitimate claims on territories and peoples we can only dream of. Dante's *Monarchia* has therefore no borders. Dante's *Monarchia*, however, describes and makes understandable a normative world with its own limits. The autonomy of the cities, the independence of the first national States (like the Kingdom of France), the Papacy as endowed with *plenitudo potestatis*, "fullness of power", are bracketed away within the world that Dante, while describing, is actually trying to bring to life. They are pushed in the area of the *strange*, beyond the normative limit of his performative description.

'Limits' does not simply mean that we know that there are other institutional orders available "out there", but that within that institutional order some kind of exclusion *must* take place.[17]

Just as Aristotle must have been aware that his tale of the origins, *ex arches,* could have not possibly been a scientific description of every city-state, (i.e., *the* description of city-states in a general way), Dante must have been somehow aware that his universal monarchy, whose origins he describes in a longer sequence than Aristotle's, was also a normative notion. Dante, in a nutshell, is interested in creating a *world* more than in describing the political history of the globe.

The notion is that Dante's *global* monarchy has no borders, and it is therefore different from the kingdoms of other princes. This is clearly stated by Dante, and duly stressed by Kelsen. Caesar's *jurisdictio terminatur oceano solum*: the territory he controls is simply described by a universal geographic limit, the great ocean that engulfs all the land. But, this does not *contingit principibus aliis, quorum principatus ad alios terminatur*, this does not happen to the other princes, whose kingdoms have borders created by other kingdoms.[18]

On the other hand, Dante could not be clearer about what *we* conceptualize as limits: his monarchy must be fully Christian, and it will last forever. There is no room for diversity: pagans should be converted, so that the Empire wanted by God himself can come to exist. There is no need to stress that Dante's freedom is never a modern religious freedom—respect for all religions as a condition for the flourishing of human beings.

Kelsen stresses exactly this point: the power of the Emperor on the other kingdoms is not described with a geographic, territory-related, image. The Emperor is like Moses, the leader of the whole Hebrew people, while the different tribes have their own leaders who decide on minor issues. This image is definitely not about borders. It is about a *world.*

The territory at stake here is, if any, the territory hinted to by Hannah Arendt:

> "territory" as the law understands it, is a political and a legal concept, and not merely a geographical term. It relates not so much, and not primarily, to a piece of land as to the space between individuals in a group whose members are bound to, and at the same time separated

[17] Lindahl (2018), p. 38.

[18] Dante (2015), pp. 150, 440, p. 96.

and protected from, each other by all kinds of relationships, based on a common language, religion, a common history, customs, and laws.[19]

There is, of course, a clearly stated geographic, territory-related cluster of political issues in Dante's *Monarchia*, and in Kelsen's reading of it. While the Emperor is entitled to *imperare*, the princes have only the duty to *regere*. The (geographic) extension of the Emperor's power is much larger than the extension of the princes' authority, but the intensity is lower, because it decides only on very general and most important issues. While any prince's authority is geographically circumscribed but endowed with a stricter intensity. The same happens in the universe ruled by the one God who controls (*impera*) every square inch of the cosmos but directly rules (*regge*) in hell.[20] Kelsen always had special attention for the geographic, territory-related problems of legal systems. The "shape" of the State, he famously stated, was that of an inverted cone,[21] whose top is in the center of the earth—something like Dante's funnel-like inferno.

While there is little doubt that Dante would have admitted to differences in different kingdoms, (such as mores, languages, gastronomic habits, sport preferences etc.), within the borderless wholeness of his universal monarchy, the *principium unitatis* implies a kind of homogeneity unthinkable in the ancient empires.

The most famous disciple of Aristotle was Alexander the Great, who went beyond the conceptual threshold of the city-state described by his master creating, via military excellence, an empire of people of different "races" and different religions. The Roman empire tried to institutionalize such openness to religious diversity in the Pantheon, a temple where there was a niche for every deity. It was later turned into a Catholic Church, and still is (the most ancient Church in Rome). Dante's monarchy is on the contrary built on the assumption of a remarkable religious homogeneity, which he could take for granted as something highly valuable.

The power of the *principium unitatis* is difficult to grasp. It is not just one land, one prince (although, as it has been shown, this aspect is of critical impact on Dante's proposal). The *analogon* of the Emperor is God himself: and the one thing God almighty cannot do is to create another God. That would be logically inconsistent. Just as there are words and concepts inherently plural (friend, baseball team: you need at least two teams if you want to play the game, and a team that by assumption cannot play is not a team), God is a term/notion inherently singular. The Gods of the Greek myths had little to do with the One God of the Old Testament, and the difference between Monotheism and Polytheism is qualitative, not quantitative

[19] Arendt (1965), pp. 262–263.

[20] *Inf.* I, 127. *Commedia* is to be found, for example in Musa (1995).

[21] "The territory of a State is usually considered as a definite portion of the earth's surface. This idea is incorrect. [. . .] Since the earth is a globe, the geometrical form of this space - the space of the State - is approximately an inverted cone. The vertex of this cone is in the center of the earth, where the conic spaces, the so-called territories of all the States, meet." Kelsen [1945] (2005), n. 1, pt. 2, II, A, f, p. 217; *General Theory of Law and State* (Taylor & Francis Ltd).

(despite the language). Just the same, despite Diocletian's attempts, the Emperor cannot have another Emperor at his side.

The power of the *principium unitatis* is no neutral force: the analogy with the One God ruling the Universe makes the Christian Religion the very stuff of which the universal monarchy is made—and the Empire is directly wanted by God. The *world* culturally trigged by the performative power of Dante's work is rich with exclusions, but it must claim there is none. Not just pagans, Muslims, atheists, or heretics are pushed to the borders of political legitimacy, but eventually all those who do not share Dante's views. It is only a matter of choosing the right circle of hell for each of them—a power that, apparently, Dante reserves for himself.[22]

Our contemporary notion of vulnerability takes shape and color from such dynamics of exclusion. *De Monarchia* by Dante, as read by Hans Kelsen, is a perfect study in case, because it strives to conjure up an universal institution, using up in the process all the power of the *principium unitatis*—and all the wisdom of the age: philosophy, theology, poetry, and most importantly a deep knowledge of Roman History and of the Scriptures.

A term/notion, well known to Aristotle, is conspicuously absent in *De Monarchia*: equality. Other political values like justice, or freedom, and above anything else peace, are cornerstones of Dante's building. An easy explanation is that, as mentioned above, the *principium unitatis* seems to imply hierarchy.

This is correct, but it is intellectually lazy as well. Dante's unity principle is operative at a deeper level. It creates a normative horizon where there is no need of a restorative equality, as all the pieces fall into place because of the rule of the Emperor, just like the universe works like clockwork because of the rule of God Almighty. The *principium unitatis* hides any possible vulnerability. The princes and Caesar will simply take care of the occasional injustice.

From this universal point of view there is no exclusion, and therefore no "militant" equality, no "equality-as-a-practice", is required. The making of invisible exclusions is, in a nutshell, the legal and political structure of the notion of (situated) vulnerabilities.

References

Arendt H (1965) Eichmann in Jerusalem: a report on the Banality of Evil. Viking Press, New York

Ascoli A-R (2008) Dante and the making of a modern author. Cambridge University Press, Cambridge

Capograssi G (1952) Impressioni su Kelsen tradotto. Rivista trimestrale di diritto pubblico 4:767–810

[22] While all the mistakes are exclusively mine, I am deeply in debt with Albert Ascoli, for the many on-line enlightening conversations on Dante and other authors of the Italian cultural and political tradition. See Ascoli (2008).

Cau M (2004) Hans Kelsen et la théorie de l'Etat chez Dante. Laboratoire italien. Politique et societé. Droit et literature 5:125–150. https://doi.org/10.4000/laboratoireitalien.431

Dante [1312–1313] De Monarchia. English edition: Dante (1996) In: Shaw P (ed) Monarchy. Cambridge University Press, Cambridge

Dante [1312–1313] (2015) De Monarchia. In: Quaglioni D (ed) Monarchia. Mondadori, Milan

Eisenberg L (1986) Rudolf Virchow: the physician as politician. Med War 2(4):243–250

Kelsen H (1905) Die Staatslehre des Dante Alighieri. Leipzig, Wien. Italian edition: Kelsen H (2017) Lo stato in Dante. Una teologia politica per l'impero (Preface by Monateri P-G and Afterword by Frosini T-E). Mimesis (Fuochi Blu Series), Milan

Kelsen H (1934) Reine Rechtslehre. Einleitung in die rechtswissenschaftliche Problematik. English edition: Kelsen H (1992) Introduction to the problems of legal theory (trans: Litschewski Paulson B and Stanley L. Paulson S-L). Clarendon, Oxford

Kelsen H [1934] (1985) Reine Rechtslehre. Einleitung in die rechtswissenschaftliche Problematik. Scientia Verlag, Aalen (short treatise)

Kelsen H [1945] (2005) General Theory of Law and State (1945). Taylor & Francis Ltd, New York

Kelsen H (1960) Reine Rechtslehre. Verlag Franz Deuticke, Wien

Lagi (2008) Il pensiero politico di Hans Kelsen (1911-1920). Le origini di Essenza e valore della democrazia. Name, Genoa

Lindahl H (2018) Authority and the globalisation of inclusion and exclusion. Cambridge University Press, Cambridge

Musa M (ed) (1995) The Portable Dante. Penguin, London

Romano S (2017) The legal order. Routledge, London

Solmi A, Kelsen H (1907) Die Staatlehre des Dante Alighieri. Bullettino della Società Dantesca Italiana 13:98–111

Steinberg J (2013) Dante and the limits of the law. The University of Chicago Press, Chicago-London. Italian Edition: Steinberg J (2013) Dante e il confine del diritto (trans: Sara Menzinger). Viella, Rome

Waldenfels B (2006) Grundmotive einer Phänomenologie des Fremden. Frankfurt: Suhrkamp. English edition: Waldenfels B (2011) Phenomenology of the Alien: basic concepts (trans: Kozin A, Stähler T). Northwestern University Press, Evanston

References

Chapter 3
Niccolò Machiavelli and Efficacy

3.1 The Prince's Ruin

Machiavelli's texts have been studied by a legion of first-class scholars. They have been scanned and prodded and scrutinized by some of the keenest minds in the community of political thinkers, as well as in the Italian studies research field. It must be very clearly stated that there is no attempt, here, to say anything really new, to offer any groundbreaking interpretation of *The Prince* or of *The Discourses*. The main goal of this chapter is to shed light on some already known aspects of Machiavelli's position, which may play a role in the argumentative structure of this text.

First and foremost, it is interesting to remark that the vulnerability figure, in *The Prince*, is the prince himself. All of the wise advice, truthful counsel, and concerned admonitions that are to be found in the text are to help the prince to succeed and, above all, to prevent him from failing. It is a difficult path that the prince treads on, full of traps and dangers. The point of view of the author, very often, seems to be a sincere concern about the prince he is counseling, so that the prince may make no mistakes; it seems to be a wisdom shared in order to prevent him from *ruinare* (ruination).

While to ruin and *ruinare* are not necessarily exactly the same, it is worth checking how often the word get used (or the concept conjured up). Just a few examples from *The Prince*: "he who does not follow this course [...] will be plagued by infinite difficulties"[1]; "He who helps another man to power is setting himself up for ruin [...][2]"; "And whoever becomes the ruler of a city that is used to living free

[1] Machiavelli (2007), p. 12; *The Essential Writings* edited and translated by Peter Constantine with an introduction by Albert Russell Ascoli. (Random House, Modern Library).

[2] Machiavelli (2007), p. 16.

G. Zanetti, *Equality and Vulnerability in the Context of Italian Political Philosophy*, Studies in the History of Law and Justice 26,
https://doi.org/10.1007/978-3-031-35553-0_3

without destroying it can be expected to be destroyed by the city"[3]; "unarmed prophets came to ruin" [. . .] "Girolamo Savonarola, who came to ruin with his new order when the multitude lost belief in him"[4]; "Those who follow the first path can maintain their position [. . .]. The others cannot possibly survive[5]; "He should fear them as if they were declared enemies, because in adversity they will inevitably help to bring about his ruin",[6] "[. . .] he who spurns what is actually done for what ought to be done will achieve ruin [. . .]"[7]; "For there are cases in which people might think a certain path is valorous, but following it would be the prince's ruin [. . .]"[8]; "He will be vulnerable to the slightest unrest and fall prey to the first danger"[9]; "In our times we have seen great deeds accomplished only by those who were considered miserly; all the others came to ruin"[10]; "A prince who has based everything on their word without taking other precautions is ruined [. . .]"[11]; "Pertinax inspired hatred, and as he was an old man, contempt as well, so he came to ruin [. . .]"[12]; "Antoninus [. . .]. Such rush conduct was bound to bring about his own ruin, and it did"[13]; "the ruins of the emperors I have mentioned"[14]; "The irresolute prince will most often follow the path of neutrality in order to avoid immediate danger, and will most often come to ruin"[15]; "If advisers and princes are of this kind, they can have confidence in one another. If they are not, then things will end badly for one or the other"[16]; "A prince who acts otherwise will either come to ruin because of his flatterers, or grow increasingly irresolute by following conflicting advice, which will result in losing respect"[17]; "the shortness of his life did not allow him to experience reverse, because if times had changed so as to compel him to act with caution, he would have come to ruin [. . .]".[18]

This is not simply teaching how to run a *principato*. This means stressing over and over again that to run a *principato* is a dangerous (if exciting) game, that no mistake is allowed, and that the price for a mistake is often *to ruin*. Machiavelli is not

[3] Machiavelli (2007), p. 20.
[4] Machiavelli (2007), p. 24.
[5] Machiavelli (2007), p. 36.
[6] Machiavelli (2007), p. 38.
[7] Machiavelli (2007), p. 59.
[8] Machiavelli (2007), p. 60.
[9] Machiavelli (2007), p. 61.
[10] Machiavelli (2007), p. 62.
[11] Machiavelli (2007), p. 65.
[12] Machiavelli (2007), p. 75.
[13] Machiavelli (2007), p. 77.
[14] Machiavelli (2007), p. 79.
[15] Machiavelli (2007), p. 86.
[16] Machiavelli (2007), p. 89.
[17] Machiavelli (2007), p. 90.
[18] Machiavelli (2007), p. 96.

first and foremost teaching how to be happy—he is advising princes how not to fail, when failing is so easy, and that is precisely what makes his lesson very valuable.

The subtext is something like "underestimate this book (and my wisdom) at your own peril".

This has obviously to do with the fact that Machiavelli is trying to sell himself to the Medici, and it is critical that they perceive how important it can be to hire him, in order to avoid, thanks to his intelligence and skills, their own downfall. Sometimes one almost gets the feeling that the pages of *The Prince* are supposed to scare the reader, to create a special concern, a fear. It is so easy, after all, to make a mistake, and a prince's mistake can and often do have disproportionate consequences. There is not so much about the risks that the *counselors* run, and this makes sense, since the subject of the work is stated in the very title.

The reasons for the prince's vulnerability are mostly the ever-changing background conditions of his political actions, the power of *fortuna*, and the general leaning toward evil that human beings display, ("men are a sorry lot"). This latter reason also plays a key role (as we shall see) in Machiavelli's way to contain and harness such contingent, mutable circumstances (implied by the former).

3.2 Contingency and Vulnerability

There is a tension (almost an opposition), in *The Prince*, between an intense notion of contingency, of impermanency, of fluid and tragic variability of key circumstances for the flourishing of the rational political action, and the bold assumption that is possible, and of the utmost importance, to know the eternal and unchangeable laws of politics.

Sometimes it is critical to be bold and audacious, like Pope Julius II. His successful enterprises were born out of his ardent temperament, that he certainly did not choose, but that perfectly suited the background circumstances in which he found himself making decisions and acting. Quintus Fabius Maximus *Cunctator,* on the other end, fought well by quietly postponing any critical battle, biding his time, while at the same time his enemies were getting weary and uneasy. Quintus Fabius was simply the right man at the right time. He had that kind of virtue that was more appropriate under the circumstances. A man like Julius would have been ruined in such a scenario, just as Quintus Fabius, the Temporiser, would primarily have lacked the impetus needed to succeed in Julius's times.

This feeling about the power of ever-changing circumstances, clearly born out of Machiavelli's personal experiences and studies, is sometimes almost palpable in the text: it pops out here and there. Some examples: "[. . .] the affairs of this world are so changeable that one cannot sit idly and wait outside a city with a besieging army[19]; "[. . .] but one cannot lay this matter out in broad terms, since it varies with

[19]Machiavelli (2007), p. 42.

every case"[20]; "fortresses can be useful or not, depending on the time"[21]; "Nor should any state believe it can always make secure choices: In fact, all choices should be considered dubious [. . .]"[22]; "[. . .] he will be ruined if he does not change his manner of proceedings. One cannot find a man prudent enough to be capable of adapting to these changes [. . .]".[23] One wonders, if you cannot find a man this prudent, and if you are not willing to wish a short, successful life to the prince you are advising, how is it possible to avoid "to ruin"? Other valuable passages, from the *Discourses on the First Ten Books of Titus Livius*, are to be found in I, 6 ("as all affairs of this world are in motion and will not remain fixed, they must either rise or fall", "sendo tutte le cose degli uomini in moto, e non potendo stare salde, conviene che le salghino o che le scendino"[24]); III, 17 ("E perché a simili disordini che nascano nelle repubbliche non si può dare certo rimedio, ne sèguita che gli è impossibile ordinare una repubblica perpetua, perché per *mille inopinate vie* ("thousand unpredictable ways") si causa la sua rovina"[25]). There are reflections (e.g., Series C, 182, 186) by Francesco Guicciardini which most famously harp on the same cords.[26] The same could be said, and even in stronger terms, for Paolo Paruta.[27]

On top of that, there are also bad luck streaks that human beings cannot really prevent or successfully face. The death of Pope Alexander VI, Cesare Borgia's father, and (at the same time) the Valentino's illness during the conclave, were events that were simply out of Cesare's control. There was nothing he could do about it, and Machiavelli is adamant on this point, that he had made no mistakes and was ruined anyway.

There is, however, a competing feeling that radiates from *The Prince*'s pages. The text is filled to the brim with blunt maxims, general rules and universal laws on political actions from the very beginning:

> All states and dominions that have had and continue to have power over men were and still are either republics or principalities.[28]

---

[20] Machiavelli (2007), p. 82.

[21] Machiavelli (2007), p. 83. The subject of "fortresses" is not just a technical detail of military strategy. It was a hot issue in the contemporary debate. See, e.g., Lottini (1942), pp. 16–19; *Avvedimenti civili* edited by Guido Mancini (Zanichelli).

[22] Machiavelli (2007), p. 86.

[23] Machiavelli (2007), p. 95.

[24] Machiavelli (2007), pp. 130–131; Machiavelli (1983), namely *Discorsi sopra la prima deca di Tito Livio*, edited by Corrado Vivanti (Einaudi). See especially pp. 6–7.

[25] Machiavelli (1983), p. 438; see also *Historie Fiorentine*, V, I.

[26] Francesco Guicciardini (1965), pp. 87–88; *Maxims and Reflections (Ricordi)*, translated by Mario Domadi, with an introduction by Nicolai Rubinstein, (University of Pennsylvania Press).

[27] "[S]ono vari i giudici che far si ponno di quelle cose che non hanno stato fermo, ordinario e naturale, ma che per vari accidenti vanno quasi fluttuando"; Paruta (1943), p. 385. See also Viroli (2004), pp. 1–30.

[28] Machiavelli (2007), p. 7. A comparison between this incipit and the initial section of the *Discourses on Livy* (I, 3-4) could be found interesting. Both texts highlight the central Machiavellian dichotomy between republics and principalities. The other crucial dichotomy, that between

Machiavelli was a learned man. He must have been perfectly aware that he was not informed about all the regimes of the world (the world was yet far from having been fully explored, though learned Europeans already knew that there were far-away lands of which little was known), let alone of the ancient times, from Egypt to far away Asia. A statement like that, therefore, for the very reason that it was not and could have not been supported by adequate empirical evidence, is a blunt rhetorical position of impressive intensity. In the light of such an intensity, all the general rules stated by Machiavelli seem not so much the theorems of a treatise, or the maxims of a political handbook, but the literary attempt to create a narrative where political wisdom in general, and therefore Niccolò's personal political wisdom (potentially useful to the Medici family) in particular, becomes a graspable, understandable notion.

Against a shape-shifting and basically ungraspable world, Machiavelli conjures up an alternative vision of homogeneity and the substantial equality of all possible scenarios. Not to take a position in the fight between two neighbors is "always" dangerous. It is always the same. It is better to be feared rather than to be loved. It is always the same. This is, of course, his basic attitude. Just a few examples: "This is the result another natural and basic inevitability [. . .]"[29]; "men who manage to acquire are always applauded".[30] They key chapter, is of course, Chapter Fourteen, *Of a Prince's Duties Concerning the Military*. Here Machiavelli states a geographic homogeneity. The Prince, studying his own territory, is actually studying all territories, because at the end of the day they are all more or less the same:

> [. . .] First, he will familiarize himself intimately with his own country and understand how to defend it; second, with the knowledge and experience of his own terrain, he will more easily get to know any foreign terrain he might have to explore, because any hill, valley, river, plain, or marsh that exists in Tuscany will resemble those of other provinces. In short, familiarizing with the terrain of one's own province helps to familiarize one with the terrain of other provinces as well.[31]

This is about the exercise of the body. The reason I indulged in such a lengthy quote is that I find remarkable the rhetoric pressure Machiavelli is exercising: "any hill, valley, river, plain, or marsh [. . .]". The summing up of the second sentence makes sure the reader "gets it". The physical world does not change—spatial distance it is not an issue. And most famously, time distance is not an issue either:

> As for the exercise of the mind, a prince must read histories and study the actions of great men so he can see how they conducted themselves in war and examine the reasons for their victories and defeats, in order to imitate the former and avoid the latter.[32]

---

freedom and servitude, is inherent to the former. I am grateful to Giorgio Scichilone for his precious remarks on this issue.

[29] Machiavelli (2007), p. 9.

[30] Machiavelli (2007), p. 15.

[31] Machiavelli (2007), p. 57.

[32] Machiavelli (2007), p. 58.

The exercise of the prince's body implies geographic homogeneity (space); the exercise of the prince's mind implies historical homogeneity (time). Relevant, and very famous, passages in the *Discourses* are for example: I, 39 ("E' si conosce facilmente per chi considera le cose presenti e le antiche, come in tutte le città ed in tutti i popoli sono quegli medesimi desideri e quelli medesimi omori, e come vi furono sempre"[33]); II, 5, where Machiavelli stresses homogeneity between religions, verging on blasphemy; III, 43 ("Sogliono dire gli uomini prudenti, e non a caso né immeritatamente, che chi vuole vedere quello che ha da essere consideri quello che è stato: perché tutte le cose del mondo in ogni tempo hanno il proprio riscontro con gli antichi tempi. Il che nasce perché essendo quelle operate dagli uomini che hanno ed ebbono sempre le medesime passion, conviene di necessità che sortischino il medesimo effetto"[34]).

Even Machiavelli's negative anthropology, the notion that human beings are basically selfish and leaning to evil, is not just the content of an empirical observation, and the outcome of personal experience, but also a necessary postulate for such universal "laws of politics" (and therefore for Machiavelli's own narrative of political wisdom): if human beings are selfish maximizers, driven by greed and fear, then they are also essentially predictable (a most interesting quality for a prince's counselor). Love can make human beings strange, creative, and unpredictable. Fear is an emotion shared by non-human animals; they can be tamed and domesticated by a rational use of fear. Greed is just a trifle more complex, and in quite an interesting way, but it still something that increase a reasonable predictability as far as human beings are concerned.

It is in fact critical that Machiavelli, and his prince, can foresee the behavior of the other characters in the political arena: the subjects, the powerful citizens, the neighboring princes, and of course *armies*. Fear and greed play a key role in Machiavelli's understanding of armies.

This means that the two main causes of a Prince's everlasting danger, *fortuna* and our human selfish attitude (fear and greed), can be played one against the other. Machiavelli's negative anthropology creates that stable, immutable background, where virtue can challenge *fortuna*.

The logic inherent to the motivation horizon is not the same logic that belongs to the argumentation horizon. Motivational factors do *not* necessarily need to be completely consistent with one another, perfectly transparent and open to rational understanding. *The Prince* seems sometimes to host conceptual oppositions not ready to be fully disentangled and clarified. It is therefore doubtful that it would be advisable to try to read the text the way the Middle-Ages *Glossatori* would try to read the Roman Law, (i.e., explaining away the—allegedly only apparent—contradictions, and neutralizing them in a system of distinctions and text comparisons).

Simply stating general rules would make Machiavelli's personal contribution no longer useful. One would just need an autographed copy of the book, and make sure

[33] Machiavelli (1983), p. 146.

[34] Machiavelli (1983), pp. 506–507.

his ministers carefully read it in order to master the power of contingency and circumstances. There is a hint to this possibility when he addresses Lorenzo de' Medici: "Your Magnificence will recognize that I cannot offer You a greater gift than the prospect of Your understanding in the shortest period all that I have learned over so many years and with so much danger and hardship".[35] Simply denying the existence of such rules, however, could turn the decision makers into paralyzed doubters, provided they are not endowed with Pope Julius's temperament. Rules are needed, but also fear of *ruinare* and greed of *ampliamento*: Machiavelli is shrewdly exposing his princely reader to the same motivating factors he is willing to recommend for ruling his subjects and defeating his enemies.

On the other hand, there is this tragic feeling of human vulnerability. A vulnerability that Machiavelli had experienced in the flesh—he had been actually tortured. The difficult-to-harness power of *fortuna* is conjured up in *The Prince* to make sure the reader is constantly reminded of the lack of stability of human enterprises. No one like the prince seems to experience such exciting and yet dreadful dangers.

Harnessing such a vulnerability means to state, against all odds, some kind of equality and homogeneity in the world of politics and war, of diplomacy and court. Without such equality and homogeneity no political science is possible, and Machiavelli's "treatise" turns into an arbitrary bunch of maxims, the legacy of his personal experiences and of some enjoyable reading. At the same time, Machiavelli needs to state his potential role. His potential role is based *both* on the vulnerability of the princes *and* on the possibility to (at least provisionally) harness it.

3.3 Normative Systems and Efficacy

This is just scratching the surface of the problem. While *The Prince* is not an oration, it certainly tries to persuade and convince; it wants to make a difference. Each single maxim can be accepted and put in use, but the text, as a whole, is in its turn a performative act, that creates a narrative within which Italy needs prince(s), princes need counselors, and the Medici need Machiavelli. In a theoretical nutshell: Vulnerability implies equality/homogeneity, punctual circumstances imply efficacy. *The Prince* itself is a political action, that is supposed to fit the special circumstances determining both the Italian political situation and Machiavelli's existential position.

Part of that self-asserted "objective reality", *la realtà effettuale della cosa*, is Machiavelli's intervention into the political arena by writing the text.

While the performance was less than successful from a biographical point of view, it certainly worked on the level of a history of political thought. It is perhaps not, I submit, that Machiavelli merely gave new and fascinating answers to some urgent, and critically important, political questions which radiated from the time he lived in and from his personal biography. Machiavelli also selected which key

[35] Machiavelli (2007), p. 5.

questions were to be deemed as relevant. The very act of writing that book was evidence of this new motivational point of view.

There is not, in other words, an archidemic point from which to contemplate *The Prince* and "understand" its theoretical content. Part of the meaning of *The Prince* could be the book as a political practice aspiring to efficacy. Such an efficacy does not rely on universal laws, but on itself.

The complex set of circumstances that determine the successful or unsuccessful outcomes of political practices may include, it seems, the awareness of the existence of such set. From this point of view the knowledge of politically wise maxims is just one of these circumstances, if a very important one. The political wisdom expressed within universal maxims, however, includes the knowledge of the powerful impact of circumstances, that sets important limits to the rationality of those universal maxims.

When the prince/counselor acts, he is therefore already caught in an efficacy paradox. He knows that his political practice is bound to achieve efficacy only because of itself, since the factors that can impact the final outcome are too many, too different, and largely unpredictable. In order to conceptualize that successful practice, however, the prince/counselor needs to, "must", claim that its efficacy radiates from adherence to a universal rule, which he has followed. An extreme case of such an universal rule, however, is that political deeds are successful if and only if they are supported by *fortuna*, i.e. an unpredictable power that nevertheless seems to have unreasonable preferences for young and brave *condottieri* (*audaces fortuna iuvat)*.

Moral philosophers have theorized the so-called Paradox of the Preface.[36] When an author writes the Preface of his book he must assume that there are no mistakes in it, otherwise he would have a moral obligation to correct them. On the other hand, an author has the moral duty to be aware that no book is faultless. That his book can be no exception and that therefore, there must be one or more mistakes in it. Publishing a book means to claim that there are no mistakes in it, perfectly knowing that there must be more than one. Machiavelli "must" offer a number of maxims or rules, boldly claiming that they have universal validity, while at the same time reminding himself and the Prince he is counseling that no rule has or can have such a universal validity. An efficacy decision has this complex structure.

If *fortuna* were truly and fully the mistress of human affairs, we would not claim she is. We would simply be blown away by her power, and we could not write about it, and Machiavelli could have not written *The Prince*. It is possible to write about it because it is possible to conjure up a spiral of universal maxims on wisdom that should, at least partially, contain and harness that very power—without ever deleting it from the background limits of such a (political) practice.

Those maxims, however, are neither like the Owl of Minerva, that "first takes flight with twilight closing in", a knowledge that can explain (or claim to explain) the past only after the deed is done, nor be a perfect expression of *prudentia* endowed

[36] See Margalit (1996), p. IX.

with overriding powers of prediction, giving full control to the future. The vulnerability of the prince is such that efficacy rests ultimately on the unique array of circumstances that describe the practical horizon where the action takes place. The general rule, used to fit an array of circumstances, would not be very informative if such array of circumstances were unique, freshly new, largely unpredictable, and/or possibly impacted by factors on which human beings can have little or no control at all.

If political maxims could actually and successfully control *fortuna*, on the other hand, we would not speak of efficacy, either. *Prudentia*, wisdom, political art, and so on, are notions only understandable in the background of a potentially effective adverse power. If maxims were perfectly effective, there would be no "game". The Abbot Chitarella wrote the famous *De Regulis Treseptem ac Scoponis*, a text with the original rules, and precious tips for the players, of two ancient Italian card games.[37] If Chitarella's tips were so good, that, by following them you would always end up being the winner, the Abbot would have killed the game. It would not be a game anymore. Efficacy is something related to a unique array of circumstances, and while it must be possible to give advice, that advice *must* run the risk of being non-effective. The world homogeneity includes the power of contingent circumstances, just like circumstances create tentative (and temporary) bubbles of predictable homogeneity.

Political practice, as a (successful) reaction to a vulnerable situation, radiate self-interpretations that can achieve relative autonomy, crystallizing themselves into maxims and rules that must claim universal validity without ever achieving it. They can have a limited scope, and the meta-limit is that it is impossible to determine where that limit lies. Hence, the power of *fortuna*.

The background of a disobedient and reluctant matter makes more valuable the artist's skill. Giacomo Casanova wrote thousands of pages telling the tale of his life, showing off and boasting about his own cunning, cleverness, and prudence. What he truly thinks about the human condition, however, is sealed within a single sentence: *Non siamo che atomi pensanti, e andiamo là dove ci porta il vento.* "We are nothing but thinking atoms, and we simply go wherever the wind blows us". Wisdom is not just trying to successfully carry out a given enterprise, the seduction of beautiful lady or being the winner in a dangerous Eighteenth-century duel. It is first and foremost being aware that no universal reason controls human actions nor their final, often unpredictable, outcome.

Efficacy is a key notion both in the art of war, where a successful military decision must be taken under the given circumstances, and within normative and legal systems, where decisions *de lege lata* (judicial) or *de lege ferenda* (legislative) must be taken, again under given circumstances. An obvious difference is that in the art of war, and of politics, the vulnerable figure is the prince/commander-in-chief himself (as far as *The Prince* is concerned), while situated vulnerabilities may dwell

[37] Chitarella (1840).

among those who "receive" the normative impulse (the law), too, rather than just among those who "emit" it.

This is where a notion of vulnerability *ex parte populi* takes place. Machiavelli establishes a link between the two spheres. He writes:

> We have said above that a prince must have laid firm foundations, otherwise he will of necessity come to grief. And the principal foundations of all states, the new as well as the old or mixed, are good laws and good armies. And since there cannot exist good laws where there are no good armies, and where there are good armies there must be good laws, I shall leave aside the treatment of laws and discuss the armed forces.[38]

Here we have one of those universal rules that Machiavelli so boldly states, "must", "of necessity", apply to "all states, the new as well as the old". The rule is about the necessity of good laws and good armies. Good armies, however, are both the necessary condition of good laws ("there cannot exist good laws where there are no good armies"), and the sufficient condition of good laws ("where there are good armies there must be good laws"). Armies are the necessary and sufficient condition of good laws.

Needless to say, good armies are efficient armies, and this first and foremost, means never to hire or use auxiliary or mercenary troops. They simply cannot do the job *(as a general rule)*.

Good laws are, by the same token, efficient laws. Good laws cannot be deemed as good from any other possible point of view, otherwise good armies could not be the necessary and sufficient condition of good laws. Good armies, when armed citizens fight for their homeland driven by patriotic feelings, are nevertheless not a neutral, merely technical, concept. They seem to imply a whole host of republican values.

This means that normative practice as well, is structured around an efficacy paradox. It will be (1) a practice radiating from a vulnerable situation. The situation will be (2) a unique array of circumstances, so that the normative decisions will take the shape of a situated practice. This means, in turn, that (3) such practices cannot firmly rely on any metaphysical truth, any universal rule that may grant them a reassuring seal of correctness. Such practices, however, (4) necessarily radiate a self-interpretation that is part of their very efficacy.

Normative systems seem therefore to look like efficacy bubbles, whose scope and duration can be extremely different and unpredictable. These bubbles are "just efficacy", and therefore they can be charged with lack of consistency from the point of view of a concerned observer, who can always create principled arguments in order to criticize (or re-legitimize) those "institutions". The lesson of the Ancients, for example, is used to criticize the modern *ordini*, but the principles at stake dwell *within* the criticized institutions, because of the already established homogeneity between the Ancient and the Modern World. There is no need of any natural law. Machiavelli's political wisdom is justified.

[38] Machiavelli (2007), p. 47.

References

Chitarella (1840) De regulis ludendi ac solvendi in Mediatore, et Tresseptem – Delle Regole di giocare e pagare nel mediatore e nel tressette, del Signor Chitarella. Tipografia Cattaneo, Naples

Guicciardini F [1530] (1965) Maxims and Reflections (Ricordi) (trans: Domadi M). University of Pennsylvania Press, Philadelphia (with an introduction by Rubinstein N)

Lottini G (1942) Avvedimenti civili. In: Mancini G (ed) Zanichelli, Bologna

Machiavelli N [1531] (1983) Discorsi sopra la prima deca di Tito Livio. In: Vivanti C (ed) Einaudi, Torino (followed by "Considerazioni intorno ai Discorsi del Machiavelli" of Francesco Guicciardini)

Machiavelli N (2007) The essential writings. In: Constantine P (ed) Random House, Modern Library, New York (with an introduction by Albert Russell Ascoli)

Margalit A (1996) The decent society. Harvard University Press, Cambridge

Paruta P (1943) Discorsi politici. Zanichelli, Bologna

Viroli M (ed) (2004) Libertà politica e virtù civile. Significati e percorsi del repubblicanesimo classico. Edizioni Fondazione Giovanni Agnelli, Turin

Chapter 4
Gerolamo Cardano and Italian "Realism"

4.1 Locks and Poisons

An author like Machiavelli looks sometimes like a knot of intriguing contradictions. Sometimes he sounds like a naïf idealist, sometimes like a jaded, cynical realist. This strange mix is definitely not Machiavelli's peculiar feature, but it creeps and surfaces here and there in Italian modern political thought.

It would be here out of place to try to make comparisons, and/or historical scrutiny, of the various authors and their doctrines. Each author would deserve a book. It is however possible to work out a theoretical structure that could help explain this fundamental attitude. This is, of course, not something that can truly lead to a deeper understanding of any of such authors; it could, on the contrary, shed light on one of the reasons these authors are still fascinating and worth studying. In order not to fall into too abysmal a precipice, I shall limit myself (for now) to a single author, Gerolamo Cardano.

Cardano was a pure emblematic figure of the Italian Sixteenth Century. His autobiography is quite interesting and useful in order to understand the *Cinquecento*.[1] He was a physician, a mathematician, an astrologist, a learned man, and a gambler. It has been claimed that Shakespeare managed to borrow from his books and personality.[2] It is certain that the boring Don Ferrante had his astrology works in his library, although Alessandro Manzoni, in *The Betrothed*,[3] was offering a less

[1] Cardano (1576).

[2] Amlet's most famous monologue reminds some readers of *De consolatione* by Cardano. Prosper, in *The tempest*, looks quite cardanian: both Gerolamo and Prosper have a spiritual entity at their service (Cardano's genius; Ariel); both are troubled aristocrats from Milan; both master magic powers; both complain about treachery.

[3] Don Ferrante enters the stage in Chapter XXV, and we learn more about him in Chapter XXVII. The tale of his death is in Chapter XXXVIII: a no-vax *ante* litteram, he believes that the plague is created by astral influences, and cannot be therefore fought by any precaution—the compassionate

G. Zanetti, *Equality and Vulnerability in the Context of Italian Political Philosophy*, Studies in the History of Law and Justice 26,
https://doi.org/10.1007/978-3-031-35553-0_4

than flattering portrait of this minor character (who is going to die of plague anyway; plague did play an important role in Cardano's biography).

His life was not a happy one, although he had an excellent opinion of himself. To begin with he was a *figlio naturale*, a child born out of wedlock; in his early years his health was not too good, and he suffered from sexual impotence for quite a while. One of his sons was sentenced to death and consequently beheaded, because found guilty of poisoning his unfaithful wife; another one tried to slander him in Bologna, until the unhappy father had to ask for and obtain a restriction order. Cardano was opinionated and confrontational, and these are not qualities that could help him in his academic career: the tale of plots and back stabbings by his peers is compelling, fun, and sometimes instructive. He was accused of having sexual intercourse with some of his (needless to say: male) students; the Holy Inquisition kept him in jail for five months (under the charge of heresy)—and he got off the hook by officially repenting and giving up his teaching post.

Brave certainly he was, and his courage occasionally bordered on audacity: he published the horoscope of several major historical figures, and Jesus Christ was among them;[4] he published a Praise of Emperor Nero, *Encomium Neronis*, the persecutor of Christians.[5] It should be kept in mind, however, that astrology played an important role in the way the men of the Renaissance understood the cosmos around them, and that Plutarch, too, had been somehow lenient with Nero.

Cardano's scientific talent is unquestionable: he solved important mathematical equations (although there was a loud, famous controversy with Tartaglia, who accused him of plagiarism[6]), and he invented mechanical devices that are still used and still bear his name.[7]

The text I shall focus on was written in Latin: an Italian translation was published by Silvio Berlusconi Editore, on the advice by Marcello Dell'Utri, a political ally of Berlusconi who served time in jail because of his alleged connection with the Sicilian mafia, and who never hid his appreciation for Mussolini (who, in his opinion, lost the war "because he was too nice"). The title of the book is *Proxeneta, seu De Prudentia Civili*. In Italian, *prosseneta* means, if we want to give a charitable translation, matchmaker. In Ancient Greek, Proxeneta was the official in charge of guests of the city state, and a proxenetic gift was given to the host at the end of the visit. Cardano sees the Proxeneta as the wise, capable, effective aid in dealing with civil, political, moral and legal matters and challenges.[8]

Manzoni let him therefore die cursing the stars *come un eroe di Metastasio*, like a hero by Metastasio.

[4]The Latin text is available in Cardano (1990).

[5]Cardano (2010); Neronis encomium, translated by Angelo Paratico, *Nero: an Exemplary Life*, (Inkstone Books).

[6]It is quite a colorful tale, as everything in Cardano's life. See Feldmann (1961), pp. 160–63.

[7]The so-called Cardan shaft, *giunto cardanico*. Unfortunately, I have no idea of how it works.

[8]Cardano (1630). With regard to the Italian translation see Cardano (2001) translated by Piero Cigada.

The book is sometimes obscure, often difficult to read, and yet compelling and truly fascinating. In a nutshell, it is a Machiavellian *Prince* for a private citizen. Cardano is not addressing a ruler, a prince: although sometimes he gives advice to the courtiers who are, always dangerously, close to a Prince.

It would be quite interesting to carefully map all the Machiavellian influences on the text. There are two themes, though, that are often mentioned by Cardano and by Cardano only: locks and poison. Apt as he was in mechanic devices, he spends some time describing in painstaking detail how to build special doors and locks. Knowledgeable about herbs and drugs because of his medical training, he often mentions poisons. These two themes share a feeling of an ever-impending danger: life is difficult not in itself, but because of other human beings.

Merito igitur dubitatum est an liceat male agere. [...] Sed tamen natura male agimus. [...] Vitanda praesertim odiosa Deo [...]. Quod si in aliis errare oporteat, erremus minus quam possumus.[9]

Our evil behavior happens by nature. Cardano is aware that this is not truly compatible with the more refined Christian notion of *natura lapsa*, and feels the need to quote from the Scriptures and to mention a no-exception prohibition of actions *odiosa Deo*, that God hates, like stealing from the poor, or cruelty against the innocent, leaving the door open for other kinds of trespass. Life is war, and we need to fight—there is no other way: *Sed pugnandum erit. Vita nostra militia est.*[10] This is a quite recurrent thought in the text: *quum tamen tota vita humana pugna una sit, nihil potes habere quod ab alio vel non eripias vel ab alterius spe ac voluntate*[11]—it is a zero-sum game, and an actual, if somehow hidden, war.

It could not be otherwise, because *mortalium genus adeo pravum*,[12] humankind is so evil. Human beings are like beasts, and it is no longer a matter of lions and foxes—physicians seem to have a cat-soul, lawyers a donkey-soul, and so on with a sharp, bitter wit, clearly fed on personal disappointments: servants, then, are all lazy and evil—*In universum memineris illud: famulos omnes esse ignavos.*[13] Actually, it is even a mistake to think that some men are better than others; they are all of the worst possible kind, although in different ways:

> Quum vero dicunt hos homines illis esse meliores, ne credideris. Ex aequo enim omnes sunt pessimi, verum alii alio modo.[14]

While the human condition in this deplorable state of affairs may look gloomy, Cardano does not blame current mores, and does not look back to any golden age:

---

[9]Cardano (1630), Caput IV.

[10]Cardano (1630), Caput XCII.

[11]Cardano (1630), Caput LI.

[12]Cardano (1630), Caput LXVIII.

[13]Cardano (1630), Caput XXXVII.

[14]Cardano (1630), Caput VI.

> Sed habent tempora quaeque sua peccata. Atque haec minora sunt quae olim, quum omnia vi ac scelere agerentur . . .].[15]

A true renaissance man, he bluntly acknowledges that it is much better now, in these corrupt and venal times than it was in the past, when every problem was solved *vi ac scelere*, by might and violence. This means that often Cardano must give cold-hearted, realistic, cynical advice to his reader:

> Tametsi pleraque falsa sint, cogita quod falsis omnia debentur humana, et regna, dico, et potentia omnis. Hic liber PROXENETAE est, non de recta vivendi ratione atque divina parte ac summo bono [. . .].

Therefore, Cardano's admonition: *Expergiscere ergo, ut tibi non desis [. . .].*[16] "Wake up, and do not fail yourself! All that is human is based on falsehood. This book is not about natural and divine law." It is not a problem of *recta ratio* (the key expression in the celebrated definition of natural law offered by Cicero).[17] It is about *humana*, about what it is human. And all human things *falsis debentur*, are not about truth, but about beliefs—usually false beliefs. And while Cardano is well aware that what is false is a clever ruse, a hoax, a deliberate lie, a subtler meaning lies in the background.

4.2 "et licet vulpinari cum alia vulpe"

That human beings are evil is no reason for pessimism. Just like we found in Machiavelli, the very fact that they are evil means that they are predictable, and this fact grants Cardano the opportunity to give reasonable advice on the subject. Love is famously unpredictable, and Cardano speaks of family, relatives, prostitutes, attractive young men, but he never mentions love. Fortune[18] is of course somehow unpredictable—although never completely unpredictable from the astrologer's point of view—but there again, such a notion is a key assumption for proxenetic advice, because full predictability would be a self-defeating notion for this kind of advice. If

[15] Cardano (1630), Caput LXXI.

[16] Cardano (1630), Caput XCII.

[17] Cicero, *De re publica* I, 25–39 (the celebrated definition was preserved by the Christian Cicero himself, Lactantius: Lucius Caecilius Firmianus Lactantius, *De Divinis Institutionibus*, VI, 8): "Est quidem vera lex recta ratio naturae congruens, diffusa in omnis, constans, sempiterna, quae vocet ad officium iubendo, vetando a fraude deterreat; [. . .] [N]ec erit alia lex Romae alia Athenis, alia nunc alia posthac, sed et omnis gentes et omni tempore una lex et sempiterna et immutabilis continebit, unusque erit communis quasi magister et imperator omnium deus: ille legis huius inventor, disceptator, lator; cui qui non parebit, ipse se fugiet ac naturam hominis aspernatus hoc ipso luet maximas poenas, etiamsi cetera suppllicia, quae putantur, effugerit". As mentioned above in the *Introduction*, I, Cicero is often in the background of Italian Republican or Renaissance authors. For example, see Palmieri (1982), pp. 62-63 (ed. by Belloni (Sansoni). On Cicero's thought and his contribution on theoretical reflection on republicanism see Sellers (2009).

[18] Cardano (1630), Caput V.

you want to give advice to human beings living in dangerous world, the danger must be real: there cannot be any foolproof formula for success. *Prudentia civilis*, civil wisdom, like the physician's art, is all about knowing and mastering the subtle net of relations that pervade, in different ways, the whole universe: a knowledge that requires experience, intelligence, and sometimes help from our own *genius* (if we are so lucky as to have one).

[*F*]alsis *omnia debentur humana*: It sounds like there is no human truth, a nihilistic self-defeating notion worth of the liar's paradox. This it is at odd with Cardano's professed Christian piety (I am sparing myself too high a number of suitable quotes); and it is probably not inaccurate to read such pious feelings as a clever ruse, a bad-faith proposition, a self-defense act, a necessary hypocrisy. I submit, however, that this issue is more complex than it looks.

The *prima facie* outcome of such an approach is quite a cold approach to human life—both private, professional, and civic life. Cardano's private *prince* should occasionally forget about honor (when he is dealing with a real prince), should be able to act shamelessly (when truly evil people are trying to hurt him), should be able to lie (when this is the only way to properly deal with a delicate situation); he should not trust anybody, and so on. He should be able to step out of the circle of shared values, mores, religious values, and see things as they are, under the cold light shed by proxenetic wisdom. He should, therefore, properly appreciate the power of *occasio*, the proper time, the chance, the opportunity.

This notion is the most likely candidate to be the general concept for Cardano technical rules: "if you want to reach this goal, to obtain this result, to get this outcome, and most importantly to avoid shame, death, defeat (whatever Machiavelli would have described as *ruinare*, to ruin) you should do this and this". This "doing this-and-this" (to be silent, not to move, to act quickly, and so on), always implies to recognize, respect, and take advantage of, *occasio* (a notion Cardano must have found in Cicero; *nihil enim in humanis maius est*, there is nothing more important than *occasio* as far as human affairs are concerned[19]).

In other words, the human condition is one of extreme vulnerability, and one of the reasons for such a vulnerability is that the technical rules that grant success are addressed to individuals, and they therefore work at the expense of other individuals (the above-mentioned zero-sum game). Let us ponder the multifaceted world of *occasio*, and be ready to take advantage of it. Since *occasiones* come in many flavors, a great deal of wisdom and experience is needed, and Cardano is willing to help.

In some way, Cardano teaches how to cheat. In a section of his work on probabilities—he was, as we mentioned above, a mathematician; it must have run in the family, since Leonardo Da Vinci had asked his father Fazio advice about a geometry problem[20]—he actually explains *how to cheat*—because he was a skilled

---

[19]Cicero, *De inventione*, 27, 40. Cardano (1630), Caput XLII.

[20]Bellini (1947). The book was published in History of Medicine Series. It is a very strange, almost funny book.

gambler, too. The idea, however, is that only if you know all the tricks of the trade you can spot cheaters and avoid a financial loss while playing dice. In other words, there are two different sets of rules:

- constitutive rules, that "constitute" the institution of the game itself, like the rules that determine the movements of the pawn in the institution named "chess" (Cardano was an excellent chess player); these rules imply a set of shared beliefs within a comprehensive group (the community of chess players/gamblers).
- technical rules, that instruct the individual how to take advantage of any possible opportunity in order to be (declared) officially the winner, including cheating.

Cardano negative's anthropology (human beings are basically evil) implies that a tentative rule *could* be: "cheat each time you can, when you are sure that nobody can spot you". This means that Cardano's teaching has two sides, inextricably intertwined one with another:

- he teaches how *falsis omnia debentur humana*, included those very human (according to Huizinga[21]) institutions that we call games: the bitter reality is that nobody really cares for rules, and such rules are recklessly disregarded each time it is possible (to disregard them safely); in others words he teaches those technical rules that bracket away the constitutive rule of the game and teach the gambler how to cheat.
- he teaches the ways of cheating, however, so that the institution created by the constitutive rules can survive: he is therefore defending those very shared beliefs that allow people *both* to play (cards, dice, chess)—*and* to cheat.

> Est etiam illud consideration dignum, neminem recte fallere scire posse qui nesciat quomodo recte captantes vitare licet. Utrumque enim simul necessarium est: et captare ut non capteris et captantes eludere ut captare possis.[22]

Captare ut non capteris, to be able to cheat in order not to be cheated. There is in Cardano neither a praise of technical rules *per se*, nor disdain for those human institutions that *falsis debentur*, that rest upon falsehoods. The falsehood is revealed by the ever possible opportunity (a) to take a step outside the circle of shared beliefs, about what it means to play chess, and (b) to act in a technical way in order "to win"—the cheater is, of course, actually playing a different game, but this possibility is constitutive of the proper game itself, it is part of what it makes it dangerous, difficult, interesting. Players are necessarily exposed to this danger. This exposure cannot be erased. Institutions, just like players and gamblers, are vulnerable. To know how exactly they are vulnerable is the only way to protect them; interestingly, it is also the only way to protect oneself.

> Ego fallendi artem et non sancte viam obtinendi non ea ratione defendam quod rhetores eam doceant [...]. Verum quia multi improbi sunt et licet vulpinari cum alia vulpe [...] non

[21] Huizinga (1938). See also Huizinga (1955) in the English translation *Homo ludens; a study of the play-element in culture* (Beacon Press).

[22] Cardano (1630), Caput LXIII.

> expectandum est ut fallaris aut laedaris, sed huiusmodi viros praeveniire oportet, quos fallere non tam utile est quam est gloriosum.[23]

Here, in the very beginning (Chap. 3) of his book Cardano states that he is not going to teach clever rhetorical tricks, the art of successfully cheating (*ars fallendi*); but it is legitimate to be a fox against other foxes (*licet vulpinari cum alia vulpe*), and it is not proper to wait to be cheated or damaged—we should act first, and to cheat such people is not so much about utility but about glory.

Now in Cardano's thought glory always implies *virtue*, and it is the best human beings can achieve in this life.[24] *Proxeneta* is therefore not just about technical rules: an idea of virtue is always in the background, and the technical attitude that covers it is like the hand that covers the flame of a candle, which is there to protect it rather than to make it disappear.

Technical rules imply a descriptive use of language: if you act this way you will get this-and-this outcome, because such is the way of things. There is nothing strictly normative involved, there is no sense of duty. It is a means-to-end technical rationality. It has to do with the *motives* that push and pull human beings. There is not yet any room for a normative discourse, for a principled *argument*.

Knowledge of technical rules, however, does not necessarily imply a nihilistic obsession for power for the sake of power; that knowledge is often useful to prevent human beings obsessed with power for the sake of power to be more dangerous than they already are.

Institutions express themselves via regulative rules: they interpret themselves in a prescriptive language (a chess pawn can be described only by explaining how you may and how you may not move it, i.e., by prescriptions). As long as you stay within the circle of shared beliefs about what a chess game is, you feel bound by those rules.

There are games where it is useful to feel bound by the rules even when one is painfully aware that *falsis debentur*, that they exist only by bracketing away the necessary non-normative background of the institution itself. While dealing with a Prince, for example, it is appropriate to put up with insults: *iniurias principum aequo animo feras, nec te praecipitem agas.*[25] So far it is just a little bit of technical advice: just swallow that, otherwise you will end up badly. Just a few lines later, Cardano adds: *Haec quum cogitaveris, nullam tibi a principe iniuria fieri posse puta*. Being aware of the risks involved, just believe (*puta*; imperative mode) that it is impossible to receive insults from the Prince. Play according to the rules—you should actually internalize those rules, because human affairs have no substance other than such falsehoods. Cardano makes it impossible to receive insults from the Prince within the *world* of meanings of the narrative he performatively wills into existence, while "describing" efficacy phenomena.

---

[23] Cardano (1630), Caput III.

[24] Cardano (1630), Caput CXXIV.

[25] Cardano (1630), Caput XI.

Needless to say, Gerolamo Cardano does not make use of this lexicon: constitutive rules, technical rules, institutions, are all quite contemporary notions.[26] It is possible to make use of such notions, however, to shed light on the complexity of his thought: The *Proxeneta* is not just a handbook of cynicism, period (it is interesting that Leibniz kept it on his bedside table). Cardano's advice is never meant to simply deny, defy, the civil institutions, but to navigate the double vulnerability of both the subject (the reader of the book, Cardano himself) and of the institutions themselves. The self-defense of Cardano, his advice to be successful, implies a weak and indirect re-legitimization of those institutions themselves. At the end of the day, while it is true that today falsis *omnia debentur humana*, in the old days human affairs could be understood and carried out only *vi ac scelere*, by might and violence, which was much worse.

First, the proxenetic advice assumes the existence of those given institutions: the family, the courts of justice (judges are "like princes"), the cities, the Princes. Next, the proxenetic advice does support such institutions by making it possible, for the subjects, to prevent those technical assaults that would make them meaningless: this, however, means to be able to fight fire with fire, and to be aware of the ultimate vulnerability of those very institutions.

Those institutions, are in Cardano a *plurality* of institutions: the city, the Church, the University, the family, the order of physicians, and so on. Each institution implies loyalty and an identity. Each loyalty and identity imply a set of beliefs in a world where ultimately *falsis omnia debentur humana*—it is about believing what cannot be always, completely, fully believed.

The proxenetic advice is about navigating the blurred line that makes the common good and the selfish one's own good at least partially overlap. This is why, in an ever-changing human cosmos, virtue is the only reality: a virtue which is both able to appreciate the vulnerable, fragile value of human institutions, and to master the technical wisdom that could threaten them to the core (if wielded by people without that virtue).

4.3 Efficacy and Virtue

Virtue itself, however, can trigger a civic wisdom that instructs how to break the law: revenge is sometimes appropriate, necessary—it must be "generous", it should not care about laws, and never be servile: *Ultio autem generosa sit, contemptis legibus, nec obnoxia.*[27] What is asked of a Renaissance gentleman can be different from what is asked of a good Christian, or of a law-abiding citizen.

Within the overlapping normative spheres of such institutions, Cardano's position is always complex: there is the technical side of the proxenetic wisdom, and the

[26] Zanetti (2016), pp. 44–58.

[27] Cardano (1630), Caput XV.

institutional one. As far as mores are concerned, for example, the wise man should show and display religious piety. Even religious exterior devotion per se is good in God's eyes (Cardano does not mention it, but Aquinas had stated that there is merit in prayer even when attention is lost[28]), and furthermore it is helpful in gaining people's respect (pious people, even when they sin, are rarely caught, because it is hard to be suspicious of them). While religious zeal is excellent, when it is faked by those who are not wise, but simply deem themselves to be wise, it becomes just a brutal device to cheat human beings, and earn them nothing but God's contempt. On the contrary, if you worship truth, you will be better at lying, and you will be believed when you lie, while liars are not trusted (even) when they say the truth.[29]

This is a key passage. First, true religion and truth worship are good. Next, they are also useful, because when you trespass you may get away with it. Then, to fake religious piety is bad if you do that to cheat other believers, thinking to be wise, but it is good if you do that with true wisdom, when it becomes necessary to protect those values that religion itself validates (e.g., that cheaters and liars should not prevail). When all is said and done, those who truly care for religion and truth are those who can be excellent at lying and cheating.

The fact that the publisher of the first Italian translation of this book, Silvio Berlusconi, boasted about his aunt, a nun, and that sided with the most conservative factions of the Catholic Church, while merrily enjoying allegedly elaborate and probably tacky sex parties, should not lead anyone into thinking that Cardano himself was being, too, just a clever hypocrite. Cardano is serious about virtue and glory, but is also keenly aware of the exposure of such valuable aspects of human flourishing to their, ever possible, technical use. Such political realism does not mean to let virtue and valor shrink to nothing.

Virtue, however, is necessarily relying on the fragile and subtle net of those "true lies", as it were, that allow subjects to choose not to technically attack them, therefore staying virtuous. Appearances and reality entertain a complex relationship: it is not that the wise man is simply able to see through civic phenomena (appearances) and, by disdaining them, is able to reach the underpinning noumenic reality (virtue).

> Siquidem (ut alias demonstratum est) nihil est in humanis solidum praeter virtutem, sed specie omnia constant, ut undecumque eam paraveris nihil referat.[30]

If virtue alone has substance and solidity, and if everything is just appearances, then it will not matter how you can get that. The primacy of virtue does not forbid, but makes room for, civic wisdom and proxenetic action.

---

[28]Thomas Aquinas (1485) Secunda Pars Secundae Partis, Quaestio 83, (II, II, 83), Tertiodecimo: *Utrum attentio requiratur ad orationem.*

[29]Cardano (1630), Caput XXIII.

[30]Cardano (1630), Caput XXXI.

Worse than an evil behavior or action is to praise an evil behavior or action, because that means setting the wrong example, and therefore messing with the (fragile) normative horizon that bestows meaning to human actions:

> deterior est malo qui malum laudat, quod malus solus peccat et petubationis causa, laudator autem, nulla perturbatione, in exemplum omnium.[31]

This is why those who sin in public seem to sin twice, and deliberately, not just because of a natural impulse: it is a kind of public statement.[32]

In other words, traditional values are to be cherished, but the power of circumstances must be acknowledged not just for the sake of self-defense and personal success, but for the sake of virtue itself as well. Cardano's formula of civic wisdom is therefore: *Honesta enim, si turpiter tractentur, turpibus cedunt modeste tractatis.*[33] "Honest matters, if carried out in a shameful way, are worse than shameful matters, carried out honestly". This means, by the way, that there can be even circumstances where "nothing is shameful", *in hac parte nihil turpe est.*[34]

A careful scrutiny of all circumstances is therefore a most important part of civic wisdom. Sometimes Cardano finds a name for this special cause/effect factor: he calls it efficacy, *efficacia* (*quae maximum est*[35])—the most important thing.

Efficacy circumstances are granular, punctual, point-like: to be able to see the *occasio* one needs to be *intentum in singula momenta*,[36] careful and attentive to individual moments, *singula momenta*.

Efficacy has to do with power—with any kind of power, and with *occasio*. The main point is always the basic vulnerability of human beings from the point of view of civic wisdom: a single enemy can hurt more than two friends can help.

On the background of such a civil society, *res autem efficacia indiget*, the matter at hand needs efficacy, and a favorable power position grants the possibility of *efficaciter agere*, acting with efficacy, and to successfully reach our goal.[37] This goal, however, does not need to be a merely, completely technical success, but hints as well to institutional values like virtue, or glory, that had been preserved in the Italian republican tradition.

References

Bellini A (1947) Gerolamo Cardano e il suo tempo. Hoepli, Milan

[31] Cardano (1630), Caput XXVI.

[32] Cardano (1630), Caput XXVII. See in this volume, *We, the People: Of Priests and Poets. Pasolini's Very Hard Poem*, Sect. 13.1.

[33] Cardano (1630), Caput LIX.

[34] Cardano (1630), Caput CXXVII, 12.

[35] Cardano (1630), Caput LVIII.

[36] Cardano (1630), Caput LXVII.

[37] Cardano (1630), Caput LXXVIII.

Cardani (1562) Hieronymi Somniourum Synesiorum Omnis Generis insomnia explicantes. De libris proprijs; De curationibus et predictionibus admirandis; Neronis encomium; Geometria encomium; De uno, actio in Thessalicum Medicum; De secretis; De gemnis et coloribus; Dialogus de morte; Dialogus que dicitur Tetim, seu de humanis consilijs; De minimis & propinquis; De summo bono. Henricum Petri, Basel. English edition: Cardano (2010) Nero: an Exemplary Life (trans: Paratico A) Inkstone Books, Hong Kong

Cardano G (1576) De Vita propria. Internet Archive: https://archive.org/details/bub_gb_XsKYeQO_FiQC/page/n19/mode/2up

Cardano G (1630) Proxeneta, seu De Prudentia. Paulus Marceau, Geneva. Italian edition: Cardano G (2001) Il Prosseneta ovvero della prudenza politica (trans: Cigada P). Mondadori, Milan

Cardano G (1990) L'oroscopo di Cristo. Officina Bodoni per Philobyblon, Verona

Feldmann R-W (1961) The Cardano -Tartaglia dispute. Math Teach 54:160–163

Huizinga J (1938) Homo Ludens. Proeve eener bepaling van het spel-element der cultuur. English Edition. Huizinga J (1955) Transl. Homo ludens; a study of the play-element in culture. Beacon Press, Boston

Palmieri M [1531] (1982) Vita Civile. In: Belloni G (ed) Sansoni, Florence

Sellers M-N-S (2009) The influence of Marcus Tullius Cicero on modern legal and political ideas. University of Baltimora, School of Law, Baltimora

Zanetti GF (2016) On normative discourse. Ratio Juris. Int J Jurisprud Philos Law 29(1):44–58

Chapter 5
Efficacy in the Italian Tradition: From Giovanni Della Casa to Giovanni Nevizzano

5.1 Efficacy at Work

One of the reasons some Italian scholars found Kelsen's "pure theory" unconvincing, was his notion of fundamental norm, *Grundnorm*. If every norm comes from a norm, and if these norms are a pyramid-like system of norms, hierarchically ordered, the obvious problem of a *regressus ad infinitum* (infinite regress) arises. What is the origin of the last, highest norm? It should be a norm, because *omnis norma ex norma*, ("every norm comes from a norm") but it cannot be because it is the last. The last norm is not posed by any legitimate authority, but it is presupposed because of the need to bestow unity on the whole system. Norberto Bobbio stressed the role played by Kelsen's fundamental norm: to create and secure the unity of the legal system. All norms converge in this one highest norm.[1]

The status of this norm, however, is a bit strange. We have no special problem in understanding that a judiciary ruling is a legal norm posed according to a higher legal norm, the source of its legitimacy. This higher legal norm, just the same, is legitimate because it is created by the Congress following those (legal) norms, much higher, to be found in the Constitution. The notion that above the constitution there is a further norm that gives legitimacy to the Constitution itself (and yet is not posed by anyone or anything but it is presupposed by the system) was on the other hand perceived as somehow abstract. Such a supreme, fundamental norm can look like a smokescreen to hide Medusa's face. We call it a fundamental norm but it could be just raw power asserting itself. Could the peak and ground of legal validity be efficacy? As Joseph Raz would put it: "A legal system exists if and only if it is in force".[2]

---

[1] Bobbio (1960).

[2] "A legal system exists", Joseph Raz claims, "if and only if it is in force". By this he means to suggest that the efficacy of law—that is, its capacity to control the population to which it applies—is necessary for its identity as such"; Adams (2019).

G. Zanetti, *Equality and Vulnerability in the Context of Italian Political Philosophy*, Studies in the History of Law and Justice 26,
https://doi.org/10.1007/978-3-031-35553-0_5

Kelsen's Dante knew very well the risks of a *regressus ad infinitum*. If every movement comes from a mover, we must assume that at the top of the pyramid there will be a Prime Mover, God himself (an idea the poet found in Aristotle). The heavenly spheres that surround our earth must end up in a final sphere which is not like the others, because it is the Empyrean, i.e., God himself (again). Mundane political and legal powers must finally find their own legitimacy in a monarch, a Caesar, who is radically different from the other princes because he is directly anointed by, well, God himself.

First, there is the most important notion of *unity*, that overriding *principium unitatis* that shapes such a big slice of Dante's theory.

Next, there is the notion of a hierarchical system, like the image of the pyramid - hell is an inverted pyramid; Purgatory is a mountain nicely shaped in different frames with the garden of Eden on the top; Heaven is a celestial hierarchy of bliss that ends in the supreme light of the Trinitarian Mystery.

Then, there is the idea that the different stages of the hierarchy are linked with the top: *L'amor che muove il sole e le altre stelle.*[3] The Empyrean God compels the *primum mobile* to rotate and to pass such a movement to the inferior spheres and finally to the human environment, the beings who dwell on earth.

Finally, the top of the pyramid is radically different than the rest of the building. God is creator, not creature (as the whole structure is). The first mover does not move at all, and in the final heavenly love *(amor)* reason and will are one and the same, because what is wanted by God is good, rational and just by definition: *cotanto è giusto quanto a lei consona.*[4]

In all the inferior stages, it is possible to explain some kind of (normative) reality in the background of the superior stage, that sheds light from top down. When one reaches the peak of the structure, things are what they are and that's that. If you are not gifted with the mystic vision of a Middle-Ages Italian poet, you must at least acknowledge that there is a power that bestows efficacy on the system by virtue of nothing but itself.

Efficacy, however, is a tricky notion. Once you admit it into the system, the whole system is somehow affected. But the point that should be stressed here is that we definitely do not need an inspired poet, or a scholar of jurisprudence, to accept the notion of a source of law that bestows on itself, by virtue of the efficacy condition, its own legitimacy.

Law, what we could call the legal system, is one of the many normative systems. Morality is another normative system, and there are immoral legal norms (Creon's decree in *Antigone* by Sophocles; Jim Crow) and illegal moral norms ("rebel against the tyrant!"). From the point of view of the lawyer, or from the point of view of a theologian, this distinction is most important. From the point of view of the efficacy principle, this distinction is at best a useful artificial tool to be exploited under given, concrete circumstances. There is nothing special about it, because from this last point

---

[3] "[T]he love that moves the sun and the other stars", *Par.* XXXIII, 145.

[4] "[O]nly that which accords with it is just", *Par.* XIX, 88.

of view nothing prevents *other* normative systems from dwelling within the same normative horizon.

For example, manners, or etiquette, is a world of its own, and one that flourished in Italy. It is a fascinating tale, full of intriguing details, that can easily engulf the dazzled reader. The most celebrated text is of course the *Libro del Cortegiano* by Baldassar Castiglione[5]—there is no question about this. Delicate problems, however, spring from a second key text on the subject, the *Galateo* by Monsignor Della Casa.[6] Is the latter an offspring of the former, or do they belong to two different normative horizons? Some scholars, because of the terrific success of the *Cortegiano*, thought that the handbook by Castiglione gave guidelines to European Patricians till the French Revolution (and Della Casa is of course included in its cultural progeny). Some other disagree, and perceive that, *if parva magnis componere licet*, just like Aristotle and Plato lived in the same century but the former performed a critical shift against the latter's metaphysics, the *Galateo* truly belongs to a different world.

There are at least two important divergence points. *Galateo* is much shorter than *Cortegiano*; the feeling is that its audience may not have the luxury of reading hundred pages on jokes and sense of humor, often directly translated from the *De Oratore* by Cicero. Number two, the audience of the *Cortegiano* is, well, the potential courtesans, those who live at the court of a prince, or a duke, or a king—therefore in a *palazzo*. Della Casa has in mind the public square, the streets, the homes—a much larger theatre. Needless to say, he speaks for the *gentiluomo* only, who should never run and hurry because that would make him sweat; it is stated, however, that his groom should do the running. In other words: common people can and should *run*; brides can and should move slowly; gentlemen should walk in a dignified way. The great theatre, however, is clearly no longer the princely palace, with its lofty halls and its gardens.

While Castiglione almost identifies virtue and manners (and his courtesan should *first* and foremost be a brave warrior and soldier—and *then* a polite companion) Della Casa subtly blurs the line between manners and virtue from the point of view of the efficacy principle. We should be "good-mannered in our conversation" (a notion an Ernst Stavro Blofeld could share): "If this is not virtue, it is not far removed from it".[7]

In his little treatise *On Friendship*, books VIII and IX of *Nichomachean Ethics*, Aristotle had seen three motivating factors for *philia*: virtue, pleasure, interest (what is useful). In the first page of *Galateo* we find out that what is agreeable is not far removed from virtue, and the reason is that "though generosity, loyalty, and moral

[5]Castiglione (1998). See also Castiglione (1959) in the English Translation by Charles S. Singleton: *The Book of the Courtier* (Doubleday).

[6]Della Casa (1949). See Della Casa (1958) in the English Translation by R.S. Pine-Coffin (Penguin). See at least Della Casa (1994) (2016) and Della Casa (2008) (with a very useful bibliography). See anyway Santoro (1967) (1978).

[7]Della Casa (1958), p. 21.

courage are without doubt nobler and more praiseworthy qualities than charm and courtesy, nevertheless polite habits and correct manner of speech and behavior may *benefit* those who poss them [. . .]".[8] The three factors are here definitely blurred.

Della Casa is somehow aware of what is going on. The law, he concedes, prescribes no penalty for rudeness, but nature herself takes care of the punishment, depriving the rude ones "of the *friendship* and company of others".

Many themes which are already present in the *Libro del Cortegiano* are predated by Della Casa, and reframed under the now overriding normative power of *circumstances*: Everyone "should also do his best to follow the prevailing fashion and conform with local customs, even though he may find, or think he finds, them less comfortable and becoming than the ones he is used to".[9] This is not just a *When in Rome* precept: the subtle "or think he finds" suggest that customs are *adiafora*—indifferent in absolute terms, of critical importance once established (right-hand drive and left-hand drive are indifferent, because they both work, but once one is established, it is mandatory). Della Casa is instinctively aware that shared beliefs can constitute a normative institution based on nothing else but those very beliefs: "A man's worth must be appraised generously [. . .]. He should be accepted as we accept a coin, not for its intrinsic worth, but at its face-value".[10] While gold is in itself precious, a coin has as much value as we believe it has. It is belief-dependent. It is an institutional fact—is another of those human creations that *falsis debentur*, that are simply beliefs-dependent.

Manners radiate therefore a narrative of independence: "even one's good qualities can displease others".[11] Actually, lack of any substance and meaning simply shows efficacy at work:

> Despite its fine appearance, then, this custom really means nothing and consists of form without substance and words without sense. But this does not entitle us to alter it. Indeed, we are obliged to observe it, albeit with discretion, not through our own fault but for the sake of convention.
>
> This is because convention is all-powerful, and in such matters is taken to have the force of law. [. . .] Other nations and other generations may have had different customs, but we have these and it is useless to discuss which are the better. We must subscribe not necessarily to the best customs but to those which prevail in our day, just as we obey laws which may be far from good until the government, or whoever has power to do so, has changed them.[12]

Normative phenomena have this structure. There are technical rules that are driven by a means-end rationality. Technical rules describe how a given world "works". This stage is not yet normative, because the behavior implied by technical rules cannot be yet deemed as "just", or "generous"—at best, it is expedient. The agent who follows technical rules is usually an individual human being.

[8] Della Casa (1958), p. 21.

[9] Della Casa (1958), p. 33.

[10] Della Casa (1958), p. 36.

[11] Della Casa (1958), p. 46.

[12] Della Casa (1958), pp. 49–51.

There are, however, rules that have nothing to do with individuals, and everything to do with groups. Groups can and do have shared beliefs about what is proper and what is not. These beliefs constitute an institution: courtship, conversation, trials and judgments, or marriage. Such institutions are the outcome of those constitutive rules that crystallize, as it were, those shared beliefs. Institutions understand themselves in a prescriptive language of prohibitions and obligations, of dos and donts. Della Casa is elegantly telling us that such regulative rules, those dos and donts, have no other substance than themselves—conventions. They are merely efficacy bubbles.

A man of the *Cinquecento*, he negotiates the fine line between the world of functional expediency, the realm of technical rules, and the world of institutions, where duties and obligations dwell. Sometimes "we must do as everyone else does, and not as we think right. In this sort of convention, it is better to be wrong in company with others than to be the only one to be right".[13] On the one hand, this is a cynical piece of practical advice. It can be even dangerous to be right and to be alone at the same time. On the other hand, the wisdom that teaches to respect the feelings, and values, of the encompassing group where we happen to dwell in, is not necessarily just an astute move. Centuries later, Giambattista Vico was still able to state:

> In my life I have always had the greatest apprehension of being alone in wisdom: this kind of solitude exposes one to the danger of becoming either a god or a fool.[14]

Della Casa is speaking of manners, not of morals or law, but this is almost immaterial, since manners are deemed as relevant from a normative point of view ("a man must therefore not be content to do things well, but must also aim to do them gracefully"[15]). On the other hand, his mind is so sharp that he hints to the fact that, at the end of the day, laws are not that different ("just as we obey laws which may be far from good"[16]).

5.2 Nevizzano's Rule

Just like with Della Casas's manners, the idea of a source of law that bestows on itself, by virtue of the efficacy condition, its own legitimacy, could be a puzzling, irking notion.

It must be stressed that the phrase "sources of law" has a very different meaning in Italy than in the U.S. It is customary in the U.S. to list the Constitution, legislation, and case law among the most important sources of law. In most European nations

---

[13] Della Casa (1958), p. 99.

[14] Vico (1990), p. 80. The reference here is to *On the Study Methods of Our Time*, translated with an Introduction and Notes by Elio Gianturco (Cornell University Press).

[15] Della Casa (1958), p. 93.

[16] Della Casa (1958), p. 51.

"sources of law" basically means *kinds*, or *types*, of law. The four traditional sources of law are therefore (1) *lex*, (i.e., law or statutes, legal norms created by the sovereign powers—usually the Parliament, the Congress); (2) customs and mores, (i.e. habits, traditions, manners; (3) the binding force of precedent, (i.e. the *stare decisis* principle, the legal sentences and opinions issued by the judiciary power that create the *common law* systems); and (4) doctrine, (i.e., the opinion of the learned lawyers). Our contemporary systems do not usually include doctrine as a source of law, although it is well known that an *amicus* brief could play a role in a complex Supreme Court ruling.

Doctrine seems, of all the potential traditional sources, the weaker. One would say that it exists only if the system acknowledges it. As it happens, for example, with the Law of Citations (*lex citationum*), issued in Ravenna in 426 AD by Emperor Valentiniano. (The key figure was of course the regent mother, Gallia Placidia, whose Mausoleum mosaics we still admire). This *lex* would instruct judges that only some ancient classical Roman lawyers had binding authority, so that you could quote only from Paolus, Modestinus, Papinianus, Ulpianus and Gaius. If their opinions were not concurring, the decision would have followed the majority. If there was a tie, Papinianus's opinion should have prevailed, and so on.

A most outstanding Italian jurist was Bartolus da Sassoferrato. He was a full-fledged man of the late Middle-Ages, completely devoted to his profession. It is impossible to overstate his perceived stature, and the impact his work had. Figaro's enemy in the opera *Le nozze di Figaro*, is still called Bartolo because of this great lawyer of the XIV century. His authority has been critical all over Europe for two centuries. In Portugal, a special legislation made it mandatory to follow Bartolo's expressed legal opinion in case of dissent among different lawyers. Thus, another case of doctrine validated by a special *ad hoc* law.

While we can find it discouraging, that Roman Law prescribed simply to "count the heads" of the doctrinal experts in order to find the correct solution of a given legal case, still it makes sense. This was the will of the Emperor. In a nutshell, doctrine is a source because such is the will of the sovereign. Doctrine is legitimated by a higher source. Law (the very Law of Citations) is an expression of the sovereign's will.

The problem is that in the Italian tradition, we do have instances of doctrine legitimizing itself. An interesting example is Giovanni Nevizzano, the author of the famous *Sylva nuptialis*, the "Marriage Forest", a book devoted to solving a most burning problem, the pros and cons of marriage. [17] Needless to say, Giovanni was addressing other males, trying to figure out if it was a good idea or not "to marry", to "take a wife".[18]

[17]Nevizzano (1525). See Marchetto (2003), Marchetto (2004) and Marchetto (2005).

[18]Needless to say, the book is a collection of misogynist themes; marriage is deemed as appropriate for those who can afford to keep it the way it should be, with his natural hierarchy. Della Casa, too, had written on the subject: *An uxor sit ducenda*; see also Della Casa (1946) in the Italian translation (Se s'abbia da prender moglie) by Ugo Enrico Paoli (Le Monnier).

Because of the quotes from Martin Luther, and the criticism of ecclesiastic corrupt mores, the *Sylva* was later condemned by the Church. Nevizzano did not marry, but he did have a mistress,

The legal problem of that time, however, was the so called crisis of the *diritto commune* (common law), in a sense that has nothing to do with the opposition between civil law and common law. After the invention of the printing press and the spreading of printed legal works, the common law doctrine became "omnivore"[19]: any idea could be digested and used, and any of these ideas could be legitimately conjured up by a lawyer while debating, in a trial, a given concrete case, and it could therefore become full-fledged effective law.

Under such conditions, European and Italian Judges had too much discretional power in the Sixteenth century, and so it happened that the learned lawyers of that time created the rule of the *communis opinio doctorum*, the shared opinion of the learned ones (*docti*). According to this rule, in case of a gap in the law, or in case of obscurity or ambiguity of the law, it is mandatory to follow the concord opinion of the lawyers, or at least of their majority.

Now, this rule has never been "posed", wanted, created by any royal edict, or city statute. No Emperor, no regent mother, no Parliament, no Congress, no sovereign power has ever dreamed to state this rule, to will this norm into existence. It is a doctrinal creation. The *docti* decided that in some difficult cases *doctrina* should prevail, overriding other possible trains-of-thought. Doctrine poses itself. Giovanni Nevizzano is crystal clear on the subject.

> Sit ergo regula, quod in iudicando iudex debet sequi commune opinionem doctorum.

"Let this then be the rule, that the judge, when he is judging, must follow the shared opinion of the *docti*, of the learned". The rule is not necessarily grounded on anything else but the opinion of one or more of the *docti* (who quite correctly found and declared it necessary). "That the judge *must*": it is mandatory, and it is the judge's duty, prescribed by a doctrinal man or men. Nevizzano was himself one of the *docti*, informing us about how that given rule must be considered as existing.[20]

Such a doctrinal point of view was definitely not a pastime for learned gentlemen: Nevizzano's "rule", his *regula*, could quite successfully spread itself in Europe, and it did.

Obviously Nevizzano alone would have not been successful, if he had tried to legislate such a rule out of whimsical personal preference, or because of his pride in being one of the *docti*. He is one of the many lawyers and learned scholars who, all around Europe, felt, more or less, the same about it. He is simply extremely aware of what is going on. On the other hand, Nevizzano and the other *docti* were addressing a real problem that had to be somehow dealt with, the mentioned crisis of the *diritto comune* that had expanded the arbitrary discretional power of the judges.

---

actually a concubine, Iacobeta. Their son Francesco was a poet and a lawyer. See Feci (2013) https://www.treccani.it/enciclopedia/giovanni-nevizzano_%28Dizionario-Biografico%29/ (In the old Enciclopedia Italiana the entry on *Nevizzano, Giovanni* (1934) was by Enrico Besta.

[19] Padoa Schioppa (2007), p. 286.

[20] Rossi (2004), p. 47.

Kelsen, facing a critical aspect of legal systems, (i.e., the notion of unity of legal systems themselves), informs us that the *Grundnorm* must be deemed as existent. Nevizzano, facing a critical aspect of the *diritto comune*, the so called *arbitrium iudicis*, the arbitrary, discretional power of the judges, informs us that his *regula* concerning the shared opinion of the lawyers must be deemed as existent. In the latter case, the power that bestows legitimacy on doctrine as a source of law is doctrine itself. Nevizzano is not a prophet who received a heavenly message from up above, nor is he the herald of an absolute sovereign whose capricious will is law itself.

5.3 Efficay Bubbles and Vulnerability Problems

On the one hand, Nevizzano is a (potential) authority (one of the *docti*, a lawyer) who claims for himself and the other *docti* an authority whose basic legitimacy is Nevizzano's (and the *doctis'*) authority itself. On the other hand, we witness efficacy at work.

The *communis opinio doctorum* is the political and legal device, that makes things work the way they work. Nevizzano's rule is at the same time a performative speech act that creates (rather than describes) the normative horizon of his time.

From this point of view the *doctrina* is based on itself, and on nothing else. More than this, as above remarked, it is—as Padoa Schioppa noted—, omnivore: pretty much anything could be absorbed, metabolized, and turned into doctrine by doctrine itself.

It is equally true that Nevizzano, while prescribing, was simply describing the law's mechanism in Europe. It is difficult to detach one line of thought from another. Efficacy is about facts, facts that are nevertheless considered from the point of view of the normative discourse.

It is not so much that law comes from facts, *ex facto ius oritur*, (the formula that seems to validate any decision taken by an overwhelming raw power), but that there is a point of view from which law and facts are not really easy to separate and distinguish.

Law itself, statutory law, can obviously display the same absorbing powers. It would be easy, although misleading, to quote those legal provisions that actually list the admitted sources of law, such as article 1 of the Italian *Disposizioni preliminari al codice civile* (so called *Preleggi*): among them there are both statutes and customs, mores (*usi*), while doctrine and the binding force of precedent are not mentioned. The reason this argumentative strategy could be misleading is that it could seem to imply the great legitimizing narrative of a modern state (the will of the sovereign, and later the democratic principle). This is not always the case.

In the Eleventh Century, in Bologna, the Ancient Roman Law was found again and studied by some learned scholars. They studied the Corpus Iuris Civilis, wanted by that Emperor Justinian, celebrated by Dante in his *Paradiso*: *Cesare fui, e sono*

Giustiniano.[21] The most important section of that Code was the *Digest*, an anthology of quotes from the most outstanding lawyers of the Roman tradition. When it was passed as law, no one realized the role that it was going to have after five centuries. It was after the Bologna School started to work on those texts, that Roman Law gradually became both a subsidiary source of law in a number of cities and territories, and a fundamental paradigm of interpretation – namely the basis for the theoretical construction of legal categories, argumentative methods and definitions, all over Europe.

The compilation ordered by Justinian—it was made of four sections, and it is an extremely ponderous and difficult text—became positive law, without any validation provided by any contemporary order, command, or law issued in order to make it mandatory.

The very notion according to which law is the rational product of a territorial state, neatly surrounded by borders, is not consistent with this key chapter of European history.

The *diritto comune* was, at that time, the most important European Law. It started in the Eleventh and Twelfth Centuries in Bologna, but it was able to survive until the end of the Eighteenth Century. It was based on Roman Law. While the Digest was certainly a landmark work in the history of law, still it had been issued in Constantinople in 553. It would have displayed its terrific impact on Europe only six centuries later, in those European nations that had not even started to exist. Needless to say, Roman laws needed a class of extremely skillful lawyers and scholars, able to find viable and reasonable solutions for their contemporary problems in those ancient texts. This, in turn, motivated some illogical assumptions about that Roman Law. It was assumed to be consistent, and the whole corpus was considered a normative monolith. Contradictions had to be just apparent, and a skillful lawyer had simply to work on the text deep enough to solve the problem. It was deemed as complete, lacking nothing. It was *ratio scripta*, "written reason", and basically perfect. It would live, in some historical periods, side to side with other customary laws that had come with the German kings.

There was no special ideology behind this (although German Emperors of the Middle-Ages would consider themselves the political descendants of the Roman Emperors). For reasons I am not going to analyze here, the temporally (Sixth Century BC) and geographically (Constantinople is the modern Istanbul) distant Roman Law turned into the successful, lasting, prestigious *diritto commune* (in Europe). The key factor was that "it would work". Quoting the right, very prestigious, ancient document could be the right move to win a cause, and that compelled lawyers to study those texts.

On the one hand, that was ancient *law*, actually the first Western Code. On the other hand, the lawyers of the Middle-Ages, the lawyers of the *Scuola di Bologna*, from Irnerio to Accursio (probably punished in Dante's *Inferno* in the circle of

[21] "Caesar I was, Justinian I remain", *Par.* VI, 10.

sodomites[22]), were those in charge of studying and teaching it. They would declare ancient law *ratio scripta* from a doctrinal point of view. Giovanni Nevizzano's rule has, therefore, very deep roots.

This is efficacy at work. There is no need of a given specific ideology for a legal or a political order, although some kind of legitimizing narrative is always a necessary side-effect of its workings, and the narrative itself becomes part of that given efficacy bubble. Efficacy can work bottom up: the legal decisions of those judges who allowed themselves to be "impressed" by some clever *citazione,* "quote", from the ancient Roman Law were instances of point-like efficacy, whose aggregate impact turns into something more general. Efficacy does not need to be shaped as a universal rule, although seems to secrete a narrative of this kind; it becomes therefore possible to conceptualize those points of efficacy as the outcome of a universal rule, and this narrative can become part and parcel of an array of efficacy points.

One may think that a key factor of this process was the special prestige accorded to these men of the Middle-Ages, these jurisprudence champions, who with their teaching started the first University of the Western world. Or even more so, because of the prestige of Roman Law itself, ancient and lofty as it was. This is not the case. The efficacy lesson that radiates from the Italian tradition is not bound by such factors.

An excellent example is provided by one last source of law, customs, and the creation of the *Consolato del mare*, the *Sea Counsel.* Since Italy is a peninsula strategically situated in the center of the Mediterranean Sea, sailing has always been a key activity for its citizens. *Navigare necesse est, vivere non necesse*—we need to sail, we do not need to live—are the words uttered by Pompey according to Plutarch.[23] The Italian poet Gabriele D'Annunzio used it as a formula ambiguously celebrating a patriotic heroism and a courage tainted by creepy nationalism.[24] Still, it is difficult to describe the full role played by the Four Maritime Republics: Venice, Genoa, Pisa, and Amalfi.

A normative text of 1160, written in Pisa, is a collection of the most important ancient Pisa sea customs. The exact title is *Constitutum usus, de societate facta inter extraneos* (Norms on societies created by and between strangers). It deals with important legal institutions like the right to throw over-board the merchandise in case of imminent danger, the rights of renting, the maritime associations. It feeds on an extremely rich casuistry. From this and other texts like this was created, in the

[22] "In somma sappi che tutti fur cherci
e litterati grandi e di gran fama,
d'un peccato medesmo al mondo lerci.
Priscian sen va con quella turba grama
e Francesco d'Accorso anche; [. . .]", Inf. XV, 106–110.

[23] Plutarch, *Life of Pompey*, 50. See Plutarco (1917).

[24] Gabriele D'Annunzio, *Laudi*, *Alle Pleiadi e ai Fati*, (1–3), The motto was, as a matter of fact, used by Benito Mussolini as a title for an article on *Il Popolo d'Italia,* January 1st, 1920.

Fifteenth century, the normative cornerstone of all the European maritime law, the *Consolato del mare.*

This text was translated into many Europeans languages, and it was used all over the Mediterranean area, and in several other European nations. It is quite interesting to remark on the substantial legal homogeneity in such a large portion of the known world. The *Consolato del mare* was used and applied in legal systems and countries very far from one another, not just from a merely geographical point of view. Even the English legal system, that developed largely independent from European civil law (based on the ancient Roman Law), accepted a Law Merchant that was basically a development of those Italian maritime cities ancient customs.[25]

In this long-lived, and quite successful, Italian "maritime law", sea-farers' customs are pretty much everything that matters; it has nothing to do with lofty ancient Roman Law nor with a class of extremely learned scholars. It worked because the Italian seafarers would export, together with their merchandise, sets of normative customs. The more effective customs could slowly override the lesser ones.

This is a minimalistic lesson in political philosophy. The efficacy condition is largely independent from any given or specific narrative, although it clearly needs or implies one. It can take different normative shapes. It is not bound by a notion of territory. It does not need to conjure up the primacy of any of the traditional, so called, sources of law. Bubbles of legal and political efficacy can be detected of different sizes and forms, in many varieties. They can last for long or short times, and only the strongest theoretical effort can reduce them to some kind of unity. This unity is most likely part of the narrative radiated by these bubbles of efficacy to claim a legitimacy of some kind.

One way to look at these efficacy bubbles is to detect, within the workings of their inner dynamics, a *vulnerability problem* that is partially addressed by the bubble. It does not need to be a deliberate process, although it sometimes certainly looks like one.

The vulnerabilities created by the *arbitrium iudiciale*, by the too large discretionary power of the judges, created the *comunis opinio doctorum* rule, that Giovanni Nevizzano was able to clearly state. By stating it, it would be re-asserted as law of the land. The quite concrete vulnerability problems, connected with the dangers and the hopes of seafaring, radiated those customary norms (an efficacy bubble that encase a legal "space", a *world*, that is no bordered territory on the known *globe*) that eventually crystallized in the *Consolato del mare.*

References

Adams T (2019) The efficacy condition. Legal Theory 25(4):225–243
Bobbio N (1960) Teoria dell'ordinamento giuridico. Giappichelli, Turin

[25] Padoa Schioppa (2007), p. 172 and Corrieri (2005).

Castiglione B (1998) Il libro del Cortegiano. Rizzoli, Milano
Castiglione B, Libro del Cortegiano [1528]. In Barberis W (ed). Einaudi, Turin. English Edition: Castiglione B (1959) The book of the courtier (trans: Singleton C-S). Doubleday, New York
Corrieri S (2005) Consolato del mare. La tradizione giuridico-marittima del Mediterraneo. Associazione nazionale del consolato del mare, Rome
Della Casa G (1946) Se s'abbia da prender moglie (trans: Paoli U-E). Le Monnier, Florence
Della Casa G (1949) Galateo. Le Monnier, Firenze. English edition: Della Casa G (1958) Galateo (trans: Pine-Coffin R-S) Penguin, London
Della Casa G (1994) (2016) Galateo ovvero de'costumi. In: Prandi S. (ed) Einaudi, Turin
Della Casa G (2008) Galateo. In: Milanini (ed) Rizzoli, Milan
Feci (2013) Nevizzano, Giovanni. Dizionario Biografico degli Italiani, Istituto dell'Enciclopedia Italiana, Rome. https://www.treccani.it/enciclopedia/giovanni-nevizzano_%28Dizionario-Biografico%29/
Marchetto G (2003) Il matrimonio tra politica e diritto: la "Sylva nuptialis" di G. N. d'Asti (1518). Annali dell'Istituto storico italo-germanico in Trento 29:33–70
Marchetto G (2004) "'Sine matrimonio respublica stare non potest'. L'utilità politica delle nozze nella Sylva Nuptialis di G. N. d'Asti (1518)". In: Rossi G (ed) La tradizione politica aristotelica nel Rinascimento europeo. Tra familia e civitas. Giappichelli, Turin, pp 109–161
Marchetto G (2005) Luoghi letterari e argomentazione giuridica nella Sylva nuptialis di G. N. d'Asti (1518)". Laboratoire italien, Droit et littérature 5:85–104
Nevizzano G (1525) Sylva Nuptialis. Joannem Moulin alias de Cambray, Lyon
Padoa Schioppa A (2007) Storia del diritto in Europa. Dal Medioevo all'età contemporanea. Il Mulino, Bologna
Plutarco (1517) Vite parallele. English edition: Plutarco (1917) Plutarch's Lives (trans: Perrin B). Harvard University Press, Cambridge
Rossi G (2004) (ed) La tradizione politica aristotelica nel Rinascimento europeo: tra *familia* e *civitas*. Giappichelli, Turin
Santoro M (1967) (1978) "La discrezione nel 'Galateo' di G. Della Casa". In: Santoro M (ed) Fortuna e prudenza nella civiltà letteraria del Cinquecento. Liguori, Naples
Vico G (1709) De nostri temporis studiorum ratione. Vico G (1990) On the Study Methods of Our Time (trans: Gianturco E) Cornell University Press, Ithaca

Chapter 6
Paradoxes of Equality: Giambattista Vico

6.1 The Philosopher of Marriage

Vico is an author whose writings seem to fascinate scholars of different traditions and interests. There is no doubt that it is incautious to try to read into his lines, in the haunting pages of his masterpiece, something that cannot be explained by taking account of the articulate, rather complex intellectual background from which his ideas took nourishment and vigor.

In this chapter such an incautious line of conduct will nevertheless be undertaken.

The main topic of this chapter will be the relationship between marriage and equality in Vico. Vico is *the* philosopher of marriage.

Needless to say, many authors have stressed the role of the family: It is possible to trace the history of such an institution in Western political philosophy all the way back to Aristotle, with his notion of *oikos*, and beyond. However, Aristotle and many others do not speak extensively of marriage *per se*, whereas Vico does.

Vico grants to the notion of marriage a significance that it does not have in, say, Hegel.[1] Marriage is one of the three institutions that mark the development of humanity out of the brutish state, together with religion and burial: It is therefore at the root of the most important development in the history of nations and mankind. The first human institution was marriage, symbolized by the torch in the Frontispiece Illustration; it was also "the world's first form of friendship", "the true natural form of friendship".[2] The right to solemn nuptials for plebeians is what is at stake in the other great change in such a history: the end of the age of heroes, and the dawn of democracy and the age of men. "[O]nce the human race had been firmly settled

[1] Vico [1744] (1990), pp. 422, 488, 542, 544, 564, 645, 648–649, 660–661, 689, 708, 741–743, 896–897, 962.

[2] Vico [1744] (1999), p. 237.

G. Zanetti, *Equality and Vulnerability in the Context of Italian Political Philosophy*, Studies in the History of Law and Justice 26,
https://doi.org/10.1007/978-3-031-35553-0_6

through solemnized marriage, democracies arose, and much later monarchies".[3] Some of Vico's most intriguing poems were written in order to celebrate weddings, like the famous *Giunone in danza*: The Goddess is addressed as the *de le nozze riverito nume*.

Moreover, marriage is defined as "a carnal union modestly consummated in fear of some divinity." It is the second principle of Vico's *New Science*, deriving from the first principle, which is divine providence itself. Finally, marriage is also the school "in which we learn the rudiments of all the great virtues".[4]

One of the reasons for Vico's interest in marriage, however, is that plebeians had to fight for the right to marry. The right to marry was linked to their quest for full citizenship status: "Hence, when the patricians granted solemnized marriage to the plebeians, they effectively granted them the rights of citizenship as well".[5] The right to marry is notoriously at the core of the so-called "heroic contentions."

In other words, to speak of marriage implies public acknowledgement of a status, and of its political and legal consequences: Vico repeatedly stated that what plebeians were fighting for was solemn nuptials. Hence, the right to marry was linked to a full status among equal citizens.

6.2 Basic Equality vs. Equality as a Goal

Here, a deceptively simple issue of equality is at stake. In a nutshell: When plebeians realize that they are equal to patricians (are not all men created equal?), they fight to have the same rights that patricians enjoy. Such a train of thought is certainly important in *New Science*. It has to do with the conceptual itinerary from basic equality to equality as a goal.

Some years ago, Jeremy Waldron made a distinction between basic equality, the notion according to which human beings are equal "in some fundamental and compelling sense" and equality "as a policy *aim*." Waldron's point is that we need a notion of basic equality to endorse our egalitarian aims, and he stresses that while much has been written about equality, modern literature deals far less with the background idea that humans are fundamentally one another's equals. [6]

While it is easy to read Vico solely along these lines, it is also possible (or just interesting) to hazard another sort of interpretation, an incautious one. There are hints, in Vico, of an alternative conceptual itinerary, from equality as an aim to basic

[3]Vico (1999), p. 429.

[4]Vico (1999), p. 208, 212.

[5]Vico (1999), p. 69.

[6]Waldron (2002), pp. 1–3: "So the distinction between basic equality and equality as an aim is fundamental to Dworkin's work. Yet Dworkin has said next to nothing about the nature and grounding of the principle of equal respect." See above, *Introduction*, II.

equality. This may sound counter-intuitive, but since there is nothing mysterious in this approach, I wish to clarify it with an example.

If I believe in the basic equality of all human beings, because God told me to believe in it, I will probably be ready to fight for, say, the civil rights of racial minorities. Blacks are equal to whites in a fundamental and compelling sense (basic equality), and therefore (this is equality as an aim) they should not be discriminated against by Jim Crow laws and the like. Now, for the sake of argument, let us suppose that the average score of blacks in admission tests for law schools is consistently lower than that of white students. Here, possibly, we have a fundamental case in which there *is* a difference after all. Let us suppose further that some black students adopted by richer white British families have scores as high as those of white American students. The right kind of toys, entertainment, play time, stimuli, the comfort of a beautiful home, the education that money can provide, the security, the warmth of a safe neighborhood, can make a difference to the growth and development of the human brain.[7] Fighting for equality, equality as an aim, taking steps so that there can be rich black lawyers, rich black doctors, and so on, becomes a necessary step in order to be able to achieve basic equality between groups. First comes equality as a practice, i.e., egalitarian policies; basic equality becomes the result, the outcome. Equality as a practice, the fight for equality, is the *prius*; basic equality, the *posterius*. Once we have given black families equal social status and economic power, they become equal "in a fundamental and compelling sense." It should be noted that there is no logical contradiction between the two alternative conceptual itineraries. It should also be noted that there are, however, interesting differences, for example, it is much easier to defend affirmative action policies from the latter point of view rather than from the former, which on the contrary seems to imply a color-blind ideology.

6.2.1 Basic Inequalities

There are important ways in which human beings can differ from one another in *New Science*. It is not just minds and brains that are adaptable in Vico: The whole human body is. The shape of the human body, its natural strength and vigor, is not a *prius*, a given, a cause, it is a *posterius*, a result, an effect (of "political" causes). Giants (the first brutish beings who lived in the dark ages) were strong and disproportionate: Their very body was different. The reason for the ugly shape and disproportionate dimensions was first and foremost a *civil* reason:[9] The lack of institutions providing hygienic conditions and care exposed children to the well-known effect of *sali nitri*. The less "city" we have, the more "forest" we get, in which children have no option but to exercise their bodies the hard way, struggling through dense woodland.[8]

[7] See, e.g., Nisbett (2009).

[8] On this intriguing theme, see Harrison (1992).

I think it is important to appreciate that Vico is ambivalent on this point. On the one hand, humankind does exist. On the other hand, "human" also means civilized, "human" also means "properly human," and the first dwellers in the brutish state are hardly so. Human nature is basically a social nature, but the hunter-gatherers in the ancient forest were not social at all; later Vico argues that it was important not to mix *gli già venuti all'umanità* (those who had already achieved human status) with those who had not yet reached that stage.[9]

Vico's work includes both the notion of the unity of humankind and the concept of other kinds of beings, quite different possibly down to the structure and shape of their bodies, not to mention the ever possible "return of a clear distinction between the heroic and the human" nature (*nature quasi diverse*) in a further stage of the history of nations.[10] When minds are at stake, the differences are so intense that civilized humans cannot even imagine the feelings of the ancient brutes: "For to our more civilized natures, the poetic nature of the first people is utterly impossible to imagine, and can be understood only with the greatest effort".[11]

6.3 Patricians, Plebeians, and Heroic Truths

Another important difference is the difference, later in history, between patricians and plebeians. On the one hand, they are in truth alike, and the "fathers" could be seen simply as clever exploiters of their unfortunate serfs. Once the serfs understand their true equality with the patricians, they begin struggling, fighting for agrarian laws and the right to solemn nuptials. Defiantly, they assert that the fathers had not fallen from the sky, that patricians were not of divine origin. Yet things may be a trifle more complex than this, and perhaps also more interesting.

It is not that the plebeians were simply perceived to be unequal, or that a highly articulated series of lies had been put in place to cheat them into submission: "Indeed, false religions were born of people's own credulity, rather than the impostures of others".[12] Religion and its corollaries—the divine origins of the father-heroes, the secrets of auspices and divination—were not simply convenient hoaxes perpetrated by a group of shrewd and ruthless patricians. Vico repeatedly stressed that religion was the result of a very special process: a collective self-delusion according to which groups of beings *fingunt simulque credunt*,[13] they imagine things and then, by providential mistake, begin to believe them all at the same time. Within this array of structured beliefs, patricians and plebeians *were* unequal.

---

[9] Vico (1990), p. 426.
[10] Vico (1999), p. 465.
[11] Vico (1999), p. 24.
[12] Vico (1999), p. 90.
[13] Vico (1999), p. 145.

In the XLIII Axiom, or *Degnità*, Vico examined the origins of heroism among the first people. While heroism was born "of the false opinion that heroes were of divine origins," it should also be acknowledged that the "earliest myths must have contained civil truths".[14] This double standard of truth fills the whole of *New Science*: "Livy make Romulus utter a shameless lie, which would have been a heroic truth if he had applied it to these first founders of nations." In a general way, "the giants spoke truly when they uttered heroic sentences".[15]

There are beliefs that enjoy a status quite different from "physical" beliefs. If a group of people believes that the sun revolves around the earth, they are all wrong, those beliefs are wrong, and that collective belief is wrong. If a group believes, say, that the meeting point is at the Berkeley Campanile, it does not matter if according to other standards (e.g., a previously accepted and voted rule) the meeting point is to be at Cody's. The Berkeley Campanile is truly the meeting point if everybody believes it. Institutional facts are belief-dependent,[16] and somehow *falsis debentur*...

Now, there is a point of view according to which the status of the plebeians is belief-dependent: it is an institutional fact. In an important way, one can claim that plebeians are different. The identity of Roman citizens revolves around such a difference. As a Roman citizen, under those institutional circumstances, a patrician is different from a plebeian. It is almost another race, and if a free woman is pregnant by a serf, *alitur monstri alitur*, something with two natures, a monster, a chimera is being nurtured.[17] This truth is, of course, of a very special kind. Vico has a name for it: heroic truth. It is a *world* of its own, and it implies a vulnerability in its very structure.

6.4 The Fight for Equality

Heroic truth does not mean "truth" that turns out to be convenient for the heroes, the fathers, although it certainly does. Heroic truth does not mean that it has to do with deeds of valor and of heroism, although it often does. There are several layers of meaning in the notion of heroic truth (as is often the case with Vico's key concepts).

When, for example, Vico speaks of poetic truth, he tells us that Goffredo (Goffredo di Buglione, leader of the Christian Army in Torquato Tasso's *Gerusalemme liberata*) acts as a real Captain does, in a truer way than any objective historical account of the deeds of any actual Captain. This truth is linked with the delicate problem of *universali fantastici*.[18]

---

[14] Vico (1999), p. 91.

[15] Vico (1999), p. 225.

[16] The key text is still Searle (1995); see also Lagerspetz (1995).

[17] Vico (1999), p. 245, 163.

[18] On this subject, I have found useful the lecture by Hayden White at the International Conference *Il sapere poetico e gli universali fantastici. La riflessione di Vico nella riflessione filosofica*

Vico also claims that the children of humanity, the heroes, never lie in their legends. The ancient tales are always true: "They could invent nothing false in their early myths"; "the giants spoke truly" with childlike simplicity.[19]

Ancient tales and poems are always true because they "make" or constitute the institutional reality they represent. Ancient tales are true because they are (and are about) institutional facts that are belief-dependent in a fundamental way. Their heroic truth is a poetic truth that creates and makes an institutional reality within which patricians and plebeians *are* truly different and unequal: "The plebeians were the 'other people,' as Telemachus called them in a public assembly".[20] Roman Law itself was but *a serioso poema*, a solemn poem. This poem was not simply describing a key inequality, the political and legal vulnerability of plebeians; it was what would constitute plebeians as unequal and vulnerable, crystallizing as it were shared beliefs on the subject.

The fight for equality, a struggle that has to do with practical matters like agrarian reform, debt laws, and so on, gives rise to the notion that perhaps patricians and plebeians are not that different after all. In the new human regime, as a matter of fact, they will be equal: they will be perceived as equals, but they will also *be* equal within the new constitutive set of identity-shaping democratic institutions of the human age. The itinerary, here, is precisely from equality as an aim to basic equality. The key passage is the right to solemn nuptials: the institution of marriage is linked to a notion of full citizenship that creates a basic equality of a new kind.

It should be noticed that when the issue of heroic truth is at stake, Vico correctly stresses the role played by the senses and vivid imagination of those passionate primitive men. I certainly agree: This is a key point.[21] But I submit that yet another issue may be at stake here.

The heroic truth is also a *collective* truth. The vivid senses and intense feelings of the men who created those heroic tales worked in a different way than cold individual reason wielded by a member of the *Repubblica delle lettere*. In refined civilizations where human reason reigns, individual human beings are at work, writing poetry and criticizing laws in order to make them more human. Reason dwells in individuals: members of the academy, professors. *Fantasia*, on the other hand, seems to dwell in groups, in individual human beings who are first and foremost members of developing "nations." It belongs to barbarians, whose reason is buried in their senses, and who are therefore able to create, collectively as it were, the great poems. There is, for example, a Homeric heroic truth, but then the *vero* Homer is of course no individual human being endowed with enhanced imagination, or strong senses. Old tales and legends are by definition created by nations,

---

contemporanea (Naples, May 23–25 (2002): namely White (2002). White correctly stresses that one of the lessons of Vico's *New Science* is that what is perceived as natural is often in fact quite artificial.

[19] Vico (1999), p. 166, 225.

[20] Vico (1999), p. 297.

[21] Costa (1996), p. 114.

i.e. groups or collectives. It is about imagination, granted; but it is a collective and shared imagination. It is not just a matter of stronger senses, a point that Vico stresses time and again, because it had been the great stumbling block on his way to the proper understanding of antiquity. It is also a matter of *collective*, *shared* imagination: The statue of Homer in the Illustration does not honor an individual philosopher, nor a single poet possessing powerful *fantasia*.

Individual truth can be keen; it can be learned, it can be erudite, but it has no creative power. It does not constitute an institution in the same way as collective beliefs do in heroic ages: It can, however, criticize them. Vico, however, "always had the greatest apprehension of being alone in wisdom; this kind of solitude exposes one to the danger of becoming either a god or a fool".[22]

The heroic struggles between patricians and plebeians take shape against the background of a heroic truth according to which the two groups belong to different stocks, and should therefore not be mixed. Intercourse is forbidden because the offspring would be at odds with themselves, hosting in their bodies two very different natures.[19] It is a right-to-marriage problem: The point is that plebeians cannot celebrate solemn nuptials *even among themselves*, and this is what Vico finds most crucial.[20] They may not marry (they have no right to marry) because they "cannot" marry, they are not equal to the Fathers, therefore the issue of basic equality comes to the fore again.

The nature of their intercourse, *more ferarum*, forbids such a marriage. To let plebeians to marry is to act against nature, i.e., against *heroic* nature. Later in the course of history, more developed and intelligent minds were to "strive to elaborate a jurisprudence based on natural equity, which makes commoners and nobles equal in civil rights, as they are equal in human *nature*"[23] as opposed to heroic nature.

6.5 Efficacy Phenomena and Vulnerability

The traditional conceptual itinerary from basic equality to equality as an aim (normative equality: equality as a practice, as an actual fight for equality) was certainly at work. The serfs began to acknowledge that they were not that different from the Fathers, and they used this notion as a powerful argument to fight for their rights.

However, the alternative conceptual itinerary was quite possibly also at work in Vico: While fighting for equality, the plebeians gave shape to another institutional reality within which they were basically equals. Plebeians can realize that they are basically equal not by some theoretical train of thought, or pondering some hidden philosophical truth which has been skillfully kept secret by ruthless patricians; they

[22] Vico (1990), p. 80. See in this volume, *From Giovanni Della Casa to Giovanni Nevizzano: Efficacy in the Italian Tradition*, section 5.
[23] Vico [1744] (1999), p. 476, italics mine.

can do so only while struggling for concrete issues, fighting for an agrarian law, and finally for the right to solemn nuptials.

They do not necessarily fight because they have suddenly understood their basic equality; in Vico it is possible to read quite a different motivating factor, which is coldly stated in the XCV Axiom: "At first, people desire to throw off oppression and seek equality: witness the plebeians living in aristocracies, which eventually become democracies".[24] This desire does not need any notion of basic equality, any justifying argument; a motivation factor is enough. The family servants "must have grown weary" of their oppression, *se ne dovettero attediare,* and they therefore started to fight against it. Efficacy phenomena radiate a narrative of some kind, but they are not originated by it.[25]

The motivation horizon and the argumentation horizon are of course linked, but they do enjoy a specific autonomy. It is a desire rooted in basic human emotions, conceived as more than consistent with human rationality in *New Science*. In democracies, the nature of human beings has changed, because it is a nature created or "fatta" by human beliefs and narratives.

It is interesting that the philosopher of marriage, the one philosopher who affirms so outstanding a role for the institution of marriage *per se*, framed the problem of marriage not on any oversized notion of nature or natural law, nor on blind respect for immemorial traditional mores, but on the political fight for the right to marry.[26] It is also interesting that he linked the right to marry to the dynamics of human equality, and to a notion of human nature shaped by belief-dependent institutions, which challenges us to question, as Vico's *famuli* did, any received "heroic" truth, or institution, grounded on inequality and discrimination. Equality as a practice is possible because such truth and such institutions revolve around shared beliefs, they just *falsis debentur*, and can be therefore challenged from within. While such truth and such institutions are not challenged, efficacy phenomena will keep a given group in a painfully vulnerable position.

References

Costa (1996) Vico e l'Europa. Contro la "boria delle nazioni". Guerini e Associati, Milan
Harrison R-P (1992) Forests. The shadow of civilization. University of Chicago Press, Chicago
Lagerspetz E (1995) The opposite mirrors. An essay on the conventionalist theory of institutions. Kluwer, Dordrecht

---

[24] Vico (1999), p. 94.

[25] Vico (1999), p. 253. Vico is of course ambivalent on this issue; see Vico (1999), p. 165.

[26] Vico was a caring, loving father, and a family man. Only from democracies on, however, (former) plebeians can feel "affection for their own blood," *tenerezza del sangue*. Before democracies, in the heroic times, "plebeian mothers [. . .] must have hated rather than loved children" (Vico (1999), pp. 433–434). Vico does not link a mother's love to nature; nature itself, the "natural" feelings related to "the blood" (*sangue*), is explained with an eye to civil and political factors.

Nisbett R-E (2009) Intelligence and how to get it. Why school and culture count. Norton Company, New York

Searle J-R (1995) The construction of social reality. The Free Press, New York

Vico G [1709] Il metodo degli studi del nostro tempo. English edition: Vico G (1990) On the study method of our time (trans: Gianturco E). Cornell University Press, Ithaca

Vico G [1744] Scienza Nuova. Italian edition: Vico G (1990) Opere. In: Battistini A (ed) Mondadori, Milan

Vico G [1744] Scienza Nuova. English edition: Vico G (1999) The New Science (trans: Marsh D) Penguin, London

Waldron J (2002) God, Locke, and equality. Christian foundations in Locke's political thought. Cambridge University Press, Cambridge

White H (2002) L'errore creativo e la logica poetica: Vico e la produzione del genere. Iride 15:513–519

Chapter 7
Cesare Beccaria and the Narrative of Neutral Equality

7.1 It Is About Individuals

A key text in order to understand some problematic aspects of the twin notions of equality and vulnerability is *On Crime and Punishments* by Cesare Beccaria. The book is a brief compendium of theoretical ambiguity.[1]

On a first level of analysis, Beccaria seems to be a zealous enlightenment philosopher, keen on ruling out any other rationale from penal law but the utility principle (an important role in shaping his ideas had been played by Helvetius, and needless to say he was going to be praised by Bentham[2]).

When he offers his insights on the proper punishments under the different circumstances, he openly—as a matter of fact, almost blatantly—relies on quantitative metaphors, and mentions proportions, measurements, and so on. A punishment in not legitimized but by its own necessity, and it does not matter if it is merely useful, because useful *per se* is not enough.

The problem is that, when we read his words about capital punishment, the death penalty, we find a different rhetorical flavor. Beccaria conjures up for the reader his moral repulsion for the death penalty, his utter disgust; more than this, he assumes in an almost rawlsian fashion that the reader can and will, deep in his heart, share it.

> What are the true and most effective laws? They are those pacts and conventions that *everyone* would observe and propose while the voice private interest, which one always hears, is silent or in agreement with the voice of the public interest. What are the sentiments

---

[1] See Tavilla (2020), pp. 91–97.

[2] *Dei delitti e delle pene* was first translated into English in 1767; it played a role both in Blackstone's (in the Volume 4 of his *Commentaries on the Laws of England*, 1769) and in Bentham's *Rationale for Punishment* (1775), directly written under the influence of Beccaria's short treatise; see H.L.A. Hart (1982).

G. Zanetti, *Equality and Vulnerability in the Context of Italian Political Philosophy*, Studies in the History of Law and Justice 26,
https://doi.org/10.1007/978-3-031-35553-0_7

> of *each person* regarding the death penalty? We may read them in the signs of indignation and scorn with which everyone looks upon the executioner [. . .].[3]

It is not just that an Eighteenth Century's veil of ignorance can tell Beccaria's audience which would be the necessary legislative proposal by an unbiased *everyone*. Even out of a controversial thought experiment, it is, according to Beccaria, an empirical fact that *each person* shares the same sentiments. There is an assumption of a universal notion of humanity: human beings seem to be an interesting mix of selfish reason, so that crimes and punishments must be legally harnessed with the attitude of a rational maximizer, and *sentiments* like this one, "that defies reason", "indelible among men", based on the undeniable circumstances that "in their heart of hearts" men, all men, "have *always* believed that one's own life should be at the mercy only of necessity [. . .]".[4]

This universal notion of humanity, which makes such potential decisions and feelings predictable, is about individuals: pure and mere individuals. The group against which Beccaria's individuals are contrasted is the family; he devotes a special Chapter (XXVI) to *The Spirit of the family*, and here there is an important exception in the history of legal and political philosophy because usually scholars mention the family in order to praise it.

7.2 On Families and Power Asymmetries

According to Beccaria, society is a union of individuals, and not an union of families. A little piece of political math is offered, in order to draw some legal conclusions about (and against) authoritarian family law. Cesare had a less than smooth relationship with his father, who did not agree with his son's choice of bride. He is not against familial subordination, but he believes that such a subordination should not be "based on imposed authority but on *contract*".[5]

On the one hand, Beccaria is sparing his readers an enlightened sermon about Nature, family as a natural formation where the asymmetry between father and children (or husband and wife) creates a subordination system which is also the content of a shared religion, and so on. In a republic composed of families, however, the children are under arbitrary control of their fathers; in a republic composed by individuals, the only "duty" is that of rendering one another (such reciprocity implies a form of equality) all necessary assistance, with the additional "obligation" of showing gratitude for benefits received.

[3]Beccaria [1764] (1986) in the English translation by David Young (Hackett); for the rawlsian flavor of "pacts and conventions that *everyone* would observe [. . .]", Rawls (1971). See also Beccaria [1764] (2009).

[4]Beccaria (1986), XXVIII, p. 51.

[5]Beccaria (1986), XXVI, p. 44.

Even such duties and obligations, however, are not necessarily *legal* duties and obligations: "Such bonds are destroyed not so much by the malice of the human heart as by an ill-conceived subjugation decreed by law".[6] There is a shared *human heart* to rely upon at the end of the day, and from this (only apparently) watered down notion of human nature it is possible to elaborate an argument against the *patria potestas*, the Roman Law institute that would delay the full emancipation of a son till the death of his father.

The notion of family is not only contrasted with the notion of individual as it were from the outside (the republic is made of individuals, not of families), but also from the inside: the "good of the family" is nothing but a "vain idol" that often is not the good of any family member.

While Hegel had in mind a good of the whole that had nothing to do with the good of the "parts" (war is a good of the whole, like the wind that blows on a pool surface, preventing the water from rotting, but is bad for the whole members – citizens and soldiers),[7] Beccaria has in mind an alleged good for the whole (family) which is not even able to turn into a good for the parts/members. And there is here the usual "swinging style" mood: Beccaria reminds us that children are the most numerous and useful population segment, and this is a so very utilitarian and rational argument, and then adds that authoritarian family law "inspires fear and subjugation", which is per se an excellent motive to uphold that argument.

When Beccaria writes that "the republic is made up of persons", he does not mean that it is made up as salt is made up of sodium and chloride. The same republic can generate a narrative of "being made up of persons, individuals", and this should prevent authoritarian family law from shaping the relationships between fathers and sons, or can generate a narrative of "being made up of families", and this will prompt either the enacting or the validating of an authoritarian family law. A given family law, however, is not simply the outcome of a narrative; it is also part and parcel of the narrative itself, is the way the legal system understands itself, with emphasis on the relevance of the family, and the ensuing legal consequences—i.e., efficacy phenomena that feed on a power asymmetry, institutions that imply inequalities and vulnerabilities. Both narratives are made of shared beliefs, and their meaning is their normative effects.

Beccaria's proposal is a narrative of equality and neutrality among individuals. Not only family, but the larger society itself is created by a contract: every individual is bound to society, which in turn is bound to each of its individual members. Both parties are under an obligation "which reaches from the throne to the hovel and which is equally binding on the greatest and the most wretched of men".[8]

---

[6]Beccaria (1986), XXVI, p. 44.

[7]"In his *Philosophy of Right* Hegel wrote: 'War is the state of affairs which deals in earnest with the vanity of temporal goods and concerns [. . .]'. Hegel then refers to a rather romantic passage of one of his essays of 1803 in which he compares war with 'the blowing of the wind that preserves the sea from the foulness which would be the result of a prolonged calm'. (I am quoting from the translation by Knox (1942). See ten Bruggencate (1950), pp. 58–60.

[8]Beccaria (1986), p. 9.

7.3 "A Firm and Constant Voice of the Law"

Beccaria is offering, in other words, an ordinal notion of vulnerability: There can be a social hierarchy, so that we could ideally dispose all the society members in a line from the greatest to the most wretched. Equality enters the stage as counter-balancing factor: "The sovereign, who represents society itself, can only establish general laws that apply to all of its members".[9]

This is the origin of the obliteration of situated vulnerabilities, an obliteration which is arguably at the very core of western liberal democracies. Anatole France, many years later, would have bitterly laughed at the law that, "in its majestic equality, forbids the rich as well as the poor to sleep under bridges".[10]

General and abstract laws can certainly formally address some inequality problems, those for instance implied in a rigid caste system, but they do not address other and equally substantial vulnerability cases; they rather hide the problem, cloaking it with a protective smokescreen, a notion of equality that ends up protecting a special social class: the wealthy, "industrious" bourgeoisie. A mechanical text analysis of *On Crimes and Punishments* will easily reveal the (numerous) occurrences and the (positive) axiological position of words like 'industrious', 'luxury', and so on.

The relationships between men and men are relationships of equality, (and they are therefore contrasted with relationships between men and God), and Beccaria openly mentions the "original equality of mankind" at the end of chapter IX.[11] This equality is specifically, and almost exclusively, aimed at erasing formal legal inequalities.

Such a powerful narrative has far reaching legal implications, for example in point of interpretation. Beccaria is all for the judiciary syllogism, and the judge should never consult "the spirit of the law", because this last notion would open the door to the legal *summum malum* (worst possible evil), uncertainty.

Certainty of law was the target of American Legal Realism, most famously Jerome Frank.[12] His careful study of lower courts' behavior found out that the judges' opinions can be meaningfully impacted by non-legal motivating factors, like, most famously, what they had had for dinner—the label digestive jurisprudence was also used to cast ridicule on a much more complex legal-philosophical position. It is somehow interesting that the outrageous concept submitted by Frank had been already offered by the meek, shy Marquis Beccaria, who writes:

> The spirit of the law, then, would be dependent on the good and bad logic of a judge, on a sound or unhealthy digestion, on the violence of his passions, on the infirmities he suffers, on

[9] Beccaria (1986), III, p. 10.

[10] This is the most famous line from *The Red Lily* by Anatole France. Things are never simple: see Sepielli (2013), pp. 673–700.

[11] Beccaria (1986), IX, p. 20.

[12] Marzocco (2018).

> his relation with the victim, and on all the slight forces that change the appearances of every object in the fickle human mind.[13]

Beccaria does not mention, among the "forces that change the appearances of every object", prejudice and biases. He does not support the harsh punishments for the *attica venere*, gay sex, because he believes that legislation should first and foremost make sure that such awful behaviors and inclinations do not arise; like for adultery, it is silly to condemn the effect and to condone the causes.[14] There is kind of a contradiction, in a legal system, if institutions that must end up eliciting such inclinations are preserved and supported, and then the inclinations themselves are cruelly punished. Since Beccaria's notion of equality (and an embryo of a notion of vulnerability) is basically a formal one, he cannot identify any situated vulnerability: there is not, for example, a line about women. Minorities are never conceptualized: he actually stated that, harsh as it may sound, it is appropriate that only one religion be sanctioned and officially recognized.

First, in *On crimes and punishments* we always primarily read about persons, individuals—never with groups, communities, minorities, classes. There is no intermediate body between the larger society and these mere, "naked" individuals.

Next, Beccaria is so weary of the raw power of *law* that he feels appropriate to stress the role played by the opinion, that *idem sentire*, those shared values, which are the best dike against the stream of selfish desires and inclinations. Jewish people, who have always been a flourishing community in the peninsula, are not mentioned.

Beccaria must, therefore, deal with arbitrary interpretations of law by summoning up a formal equality narrative, one that implies a "firm and constant voice of the law", able to override "the erroneous instability of interpretations". This notion of a law endowed with a *firm and constant voice* is part and parcel of the narrative: such a law and such a voice exist only within such a narrative.[15]

The notion that a norm can have a single, correct, inherent meaning, that pits it against other possible but erroneous meanings, which are merely the outcome of an interpretation process (not really necessary when apprehending the real and unique meaning of the norm itself), is, at best, controversial.

Even if we assume, for the sake of the argument, that a literal (and therefore not based on the "spirit") meaning of the norm does exist, the decision to choose that literal meaning is itself an interpretation fact. Zero is a number like the others, there is no qualitative difference, no *per saltum* distinction, between the meaning of a norm as an outcome of a literal interpretation and the meaning of a norm as an outcome of other kinds of interpretation. While some interpretation processes may seem to be more articulate than others, there is no dichotomy involved: interpretation is inherent to any normative segment that dwells within a given institutional horizon. Judicial decisions, like legislative decisions, are but punctual efficacy phenomena; they radiate, of course, their own self-legitimizing narrative, which is the other side

[13] Beccaria (1986), IV, p. 11.

[14] Beccaria (1986), XXXI, p. 60.

[15] Beccaria (1986), IV, p. 11.

of the phenomena per se, where the distance between "motivation" and "argumentation" can be more or less wide.

It is worth remarking that Beccaria has a functional, not a structural, concept of such a notion: the firm and constant voice is simply an overriding interpretation that, because it is linked with efficacy phenomena in the courts, makes it possible to anticipate the legal outcomes of any behavior—the punishment that will follow a given crime, and so on. Such a firm and constant voice is never described per se: laws must be as simple and easy to understand as they can be because of this reason, that the firm and constant voice must be taken for granted. Having said so, *any interpretation* that is able to override any possible alternative one, therefore being liable to be thought of as *the* correct meaning inherent to that norm, will be deemed as the *firm and constant voice*.

Beccaria is simply stating that a more stable and predictable efficacy bubble would be quite useful to those subjects who are eager to live their industrious, productive, wealthy and luxurious life. Since his book is a performative act that should (and did) nudge into existence the narrative that would substantiate such a bubble—such an enlightened reformed legal system--, from within such a narrative he fought against capricious and arbitrary judiciary decisions, asking for general laws able to prevent whimsical and "digestive" legal violence.

7.4 Efficacy and Pluralism

Even *On Crimes and Punishments*, however, at the end of the day acknowledges (although in an embryonic and perhaps uncertain way) the pluralism that seems inherent in the efficacy principle. Efficacy is not bound to create unity-endowed systems: we have actually only efficacy phenomena, that are more or less arbitrarily subsumed into a system by a narrative that radiates from the phenomena themselves. The narrative is exactly that which allows the observer to perceive them as such, i.e., as efficacy phenomena—they would not exist *per se*, but co-exist with a narrative, no matter how crude, that is not just a noetic condition for their understanding, but also an alethic condition for their existence; the narrative, on the other hand, exists because of them, and has no other status or function than to make those phenomena intelligible and existing *as efficacy phenomena.* This means that legal systems are impure from more than one point of view, because their narrative must imply an overriding power (inherent in their identity) on other narratives, that must therefore exist for those systems whose *raison d'etre* is the vanishing (from any relevant efficacy horizon) of such mentioned alternative narratives.

Beccaria finds a bubble which is resisting his own, and acknowledges it with adamant intellectual honesty. The spell is lifted for a moment. The alternative narrative has a name, *honor*, and the problem is addressed in chapter IX and X of the book.

Honor is something that is not related to industrious and productive subjects; it has nothing to do with property and wealth. It is not even a universal notion, because plebeians do not duel. It can lead to crime, but it is a crime committed following an unwritten code of rules, rules that revolve around ancient and established principles. Above all, honor rules have on their side the power of opinion, something Beccaria can never underestimate.

It takes two to duel, and therefore there is a shared legal responsibility. Beccaria, however, following a mainstream opinion in his social circle, recommends a punishment only for the aggressor, i.e., for he who created the occasion (offence) for the duel. The dueler who is not an aggressor, says Beccaria, should not be punished at all, he simply shows that he fears only the law, and not the other man.[16] In other words, Beccaria does acknowledge that honor is indeed a problem, and while it is regrettable that some disrespectful subjects initiate a process that has to end up with a duel, still the honor-linked efficacy phenomena cannot be dismissed and the legal system must somehow acknowledge them even if their narrative is incompatible with its own.

> Edicts threatening death to anyone who accepts a challenge to duel have vainly sought to extirpate this custom, which is founded on something that some men fear more than death.[17]

The legal system loses efficacy faced by an alternative efficacy bubble, for a *custom* is indeed a normative segment endowed with its own efficacy power, founded on *something* that is extraneous to the narrative of the system. This is why Beccaria joins forces with those who believe that he should be deemed as innocent who simply found himself forced to defend *something* that "laws on the books" (i.e., the legal system) do not assure to him. Such a something is "the opinion the others hold" of him, but it is not a neutral opinion, or liable to be comprehended with the narrative of the legal system. It is an opinion that has to do with honor and bravery, with a special self-respect that somehow borders on a legitimate pride, sometimes close to a courageous boldness. There is a whole dictionary that makes perfect sense only within the narrative of honor. It is not necessarily compatible with the official legal narrative. Nevertheless, the latter must acknowledge the former in order to neutralize the unspeakable, embarrassing principle: efficacy phenomena are never harnessed by any narrative, although narratives must imply that they can and do just that.

Since efficacy phenomena and their narratives are coexistent, and neither has any kind of reality without the other, Beccaria is actually cooperating to the creation/support of a given narrative that can and will have legal consequences: the Enlightenment reform program.

The most famous part of such a program concerns the abolition of torture and a severe restriction of death penalty. Michel Foucault correctly argued that Beccaria's program was not about diminishing the disciplinary power of European societies, it

[16] Beccaria (1986), IX-X, pp. 19–21.

[17] Beccaria (1986), X, p. 21.

was about extending, while at the same time de-intensifying, it. The age of the prison system was dawning.[18]

Beccaria's demands are quite high. In order to diminish the *cruelty* of punishments, it is necessary to increase their *inevitability*. The power to endow punishment with inevitability, promptness, and duration must be very high indeed, and implies a perfect social control.

This is one of the passages in *On Crimes and Punishments* where more visible is Beccaria's ambiguous struggling with the performative logic of efficacy phenomena. On the one hand he says that "all laws which conflict with natural human feelings are useless and consequently dangerous".[19] That would perhaps apply to the duel problem, although the subject matter, in this case, are oaths, in Chapter XVIII. This insistence on shared opinions, on feelings, give sometimes to Beccaria's prose an almost Burkean flavor. This is not, however, the case, because Beccaria does not believe in the sanction of time. Traditions, even ancient and universal traditions, can be wrong.

What Augustine says of sodomy, that it would be wrong even if everybody would approve of it, Beccaria states about the death penalty: it does not matter that the institution had an extraordinary success, and was widespread among all known people and nations—so were human sacrifice as well. One should assume that behind executions and human sacrifices there are important human feelings, *a là* Bataille in *The Tears of Eros*.[20] All of a sudden, however, valuable and cherished shared feelings turn into "the hue and cry of so many people who are guided by blind habit", a force against which "the voice of one philosopher" cannot unfortunately prevail. It could prevail, however, if that one philosopher could take care that such an inconvenient truth would reach "the throne of monarch"—the enlightened despot could then make the appropriate changes and at that point *it would become real* that such a Truth "comes with the secret desires of all men"—in other words, the narrative and the efficacy phenomena would change together. This is a way to look at Beccaria's leanings toward enlightened, benevolent despotism.

References

Bataille G (1961) Le larmes d'Éros. English edition: Bataille G (1989) The tears of eros (trans: Connor P). City Lights Books, San Francisco

Beccaria C [1764] Dei delitti e delle pene. English edition: Beccaria C (1986) On crimes and punishments (trans: Young D). Hackett, Indianapolis

[18]Foucault [1961] (1979) in the English translation by Sheridan (Vintage Books), pp. 81–82. According to Angelo Bellini, however, Gerolamo Cardano had already questioned both torture and death penalty. See Bellini (1947), p. 197.

[19]Beccaria (1986), XVIII, p. 35.

[20]Bataille [1961] (1989) in the English translation by Peter Connor (City Lights Books).

Beccaria C [1764] Dei delitti e delle pene. English edition: Beccaria C (1986) On crimes and punishments and other writings (trans: Thomas A). University of Toronto Press, Toronto
Bellini A (1947) Gerolamo Cardano e il suo tempo. Ulrico Hoepli, Milan
Hart H-L-A (1982) Essays on Bentham: Jurisprudence and political philosophy. Oxford University Press, Oxford
Hegel G-W-F (1821) Grundlinien der Philosophie des Rechts. Berlino. English edition: Hegel G-W-F (1942) Hegel's Philosophy of right (trans: Knox T-M). Oxford University Press, London
Marzocco V (2018) Nella mente del giudice. Il contributo di Jerome Frank al realismo giuridico Americano. Giappichelli, Turin
Rawls J (1971) A theory of justice. Oxford University Press, Oxford
Sepielli A (2013) The law's 'majestic equality. Law Philos 32:673–700
Tavilla C-E (2020) Beccaria nella rilettura della scienza giuridica italiana più recente. Revue d'histoire du droit de punir 91–97
ten Bruggencate H-G (1950) Hegel's views on war. Philos Quart 1(1):58–60

Chapter 8
Equality and Vulnerability in *The Duties of Man*: Giuseppe Mazzini

8.1 An Idiosyncratic Reading

It is quite difficult, and almost impossible, to disentangle Giuseppe Mazzini from the multi-layered net of interpretations that have created the Mazzini myth. In Italian schoolbooks, he was almost a bidimensional figure of a Risorgimento hero: the purest republican politician, the never-smiling patriot,[1] the inspired, although almost *disarmato,* prophet.

There is a complexity in Mazzini that defies and challenges most of the traditional images that were passed down with an almost religious awe. High school students of my generation were never told, of course, that the noblest *padre della patria* was a strong, unapologetic advocate of the rights of women, and that he deemed the subjugation of women one of the worst crimes of his time. The problem was that in the sixties and seventies Mazzini's position on the subject was still a tad too radical, and potentially at odds with some of the presumptive shared values that were inspiring more than a few political and intellectual actors of the time. [2]

There is still controversy about his membership in freemasonry. He certainly plotted with the *Carboneria*, a patriotic secret society: freemasonry is, however, another kettle of fish, because it is still a living (and, at least in Italy, somehow controversial) institution. Mazzini's fondness for music was not deemed important in the old days, and his interest in Asian religion (and for the idea of reincarnation) is not a subject matter that Mazzini worshippers must have been comfortable with.[3] Religion is a key notion in the thought of the so-called Apostle, but that did not

[1]Giosuè Carducci, *Giambi ed Epodi* [1906], II, XXIII, *Giuseppe Mazzini,* v. 13: "il volto che giammai non rise".

[2]The standard biography is still Mack Smith (1996); see also Dal Lago (2013) or Urbinati (2012), pp. 183–204 or Recchia and Urbinati (2009).

[3]Mazzini [1841–1871] (2011).

G. Zanetti, *Equality and Vulnerability in the Context of Italian Political Philosophy*, Studies in the History of Law and Justice 26,
https://doi.org/10.1007/978-3-031-35553-0_8

prevent him from being a fierce enemy of the Catholic Church, both from a political and a theological point of view. He spent all of his life plotting and fighting, mostly unsuccessfully, and struggling over the overlapping problems of Italian Unity and the social question.

Mazzini spent most of his life abroad, in exile, sometimes in a dire financial situation, but was eventually able to die in Pisa, where he would live under the pseudonym of John Brown: it was, most likely, a homage to the American abolitionist hero of the Underground Railroad.

Mazzini was a man of the Nineteenth Century. His writing style is somehow hard to digest, full as it is of a no longer fashionable romantic rhetoric. His somewhat patronizing admonitions, his well-meaning sound and fury, can be quite difficult to swallow.

The Duties of Man is one of his best-known books. It is, also, a short book: it was meant to be the republican counterpart of *The Communist Manifesto* by Marx and Engels; its ideal audience was the community of Italian poor workers. It is, therefore, a (deceptively) easy, smooth text: there is a surface meaning quite easy to grasp.[4]

There are, however, deeper layers of meaning, and it is obviously not possible to scrutinize all of them now. As a matter of fact, it is not relevant to this course aim to delve into the historical and philological details of the book, nor even to analyze or imagine what Mazzini "really" thought or meant. Our effort will be to analyze the text per se, in order to detect in it key themes that are relevant to our research project, themes that seem to surface in the text, possibly without the author being aware of their untapped potential.

This implies an idiosyncratic reading, a deliberately one-sided analysis. The text will be arbitrarily exposed to and analyzed through some theoretical questions, in order to see and check the chemical reaction in terms of legal and political philosophy, therefore without truly scanning Giuseppe Mazzini's own real-and-personal point of view, but just the normative reasoning possibly inherent in the text. While such a method is certainly not to be recommended to any Mazzini scholar, and it would be out of place in an essay about "Giuseppe Mazzini" as an historical figure, it is perfectly useful when one tries to detect the emergence of philosophical themes, relevant from the researcher's point of view, that often elude their own author, popping out of his text almost *malgré lui*.

---

[4]Mazzini [1860] (1862) in the English translation by Emile Ashurst Venturi (Chapman & Hall). I am quoting from The Kessinger Publishing's Rare Reprints. Karl Marx, most famously, harshly criticized Mazzini.

8.2 God as a Self-Defeating Concept

First, it could be stressed that the theme of equality is central in Mazzini's train-of-thought: it is mentioned on the first page, the *Preface to the Italian Working Class.*[5] On the one hand Mazzini says that he thought of the *sufferings* of poor Italians, and on the other he frankly admits that "unjust inequalities now so fatal to the free development" of the people's *faculties*, must be overcome.[6] Communist theories were already thriving in Europe, much to Mazzini's chagrin, and his notion of equality had to address the issue of distributive justice: "Why then has not the condition of the people improved? Why has the consumption of produce – instead of being equally distributed among all members of European Society – become concentrated in the hands of a few, of a class forming a new aristocracy?".[7] The main shortcoming of a life of poverty, in Mazzini's eyes, is that it makes it basically impossible to fulfill one's potential,[8] to develop oneself, and when this lofty goal is forgotten the selfish individual falls into what he calls egotism, i.e., the attitude of a rational maximizer unaware of the broader meaning radiating from a social and cultural progress that can flourish only by validating communities like the family, the nation, and humanity itself (all notions that in Mazzini are consistently written in upper case). The awareness of such a broader meaning implies the key role played by the notion of human duties, that do not erase human rights, but makes sure that the latter do not degenerate into such an individualistic egotism.[9]

In order to provide a firm foundation for this ambitious normative program, Mazzini has no qualms in conjuring up a notion of God: "There are, I hope, no atheists among you".[10] He had been under the Jansenist influence of his devout mother, true, and he might have even perceived how unprofitable it would have been to leave the powerful religious narrative in the hands of a conservative aristocracy, an alliance "between throne and altar"—to predate that narrative, and to claim for the progressive and subversive republicans the glorious halo of true religion, was and still is a clever political move. But this is exactly the kind of analysis we are not interested in here. I submit that, in the text of The *Duties of Man*, the notion of God is a self-defeating concept, i.e. a concept with no content whatsoever whose only structural meaning is to make possible a normative discourse which specifically does not need any idea of God.

First, the notion of God is a condition for the flourishing of a normative discourse:

[5]Monarchy as a form of government represents a serious violation of the principle of equality between human beings; this is one of the main reasons for Mazzini's republican "option".

[6]Mazzini (1862), p. IX.

[7]Mazzini (1862), p. 7.

[8]This idea is still active in the Italian Constitution, art. 3, second paragraph.

[9]The notion of duties is still active in the Italian republican tradition, as in Viroli (2008).

[10]Mazzini (1862), p. 31.

> We must either obey God or serve man; whether one man or many, matters little. [. . .] If there be not one holy inviolable Law, uncreated by man, what rule have we by which to judge whether a given act be just or unjust?
>
> In the name of whom or of what shall we protest against inequality and oppression?
>
> Without God there is no other rule than that of *Fact*, the accomplished Fact [. . .].[11]

The goal here is clearly stated: to be able "to judge", i.e., to criticize, to either legitimate or to prove not legitimate a given act, where the rationale is "not to serve man". God, on the other hand, is here an assumption of a non-individualistic background, i.e. a providential set of shared beliefs. These beliefs are the only reason God seems to exist in Mazzini's cosmos: they have a lofty name, the Law of God.

In a Vichian[12] way, without the knowledge of this Law "you may not pretend to the name or the rights of men".[13] It is not that a natural law is responsible for making human beings "real men", it is rather necessary to reach a point of awareness, of knowledge of such Law, in order to deserve the name of men, which is tantamount to claim that human beings are truly human when they find out this law, that has this basic meaning, to make them human.

The content of this humanity, however, is simply the fight against oppression and inequality: The Law of God is "defence against the unjust laws".[14]

There is no given scriptural fixed content:

> Those who declare that the *whole* moral is contained in a book, or uttered by one man, forget that there is no single code of morals which Humanity has not abandoned, after an acceptance and belief of some centuries, in order to seek after and diffuse another more advanced than it; nor is there any special reason for supposing that Humanity will alter its course now.[15]

In other words, each historical religious-based morality, or politics, is only contingently relevant, and its deeper meaning is to be a better (*more advanced*) system than the one it criticizes. This means that normative institutions based on Mazzini's God and his lofty Law & Religion are inherently exposed to a critique radiating by the very principles that give to those institutions their contingent legitimacy: fighting and arguing against inequality and oppression. This includes not just the present state of affairs, but Mazzini's own religious ideas: *there is certainly no special reason for supposing that humanity will alter its course.*

---

[11] Mazzini (1862), p. 47.

[12] The notion that (true) humanity is an arrival point, not a departure time, is in Vico linked with the idea of education, whereby it becomes possible to *e-ducere*, to somehow extract, that humanity from the darkness where dwell the *uman bestioni*.

[13] Mazzini (1862), pp. 50–51.

[14] As Tommaso Greco reminds me, God as a guarantee of human freedom is certainly no novelty. See Mathieu (1989) on Thomas More.

[15] Mazzini (1862), p. 52.

8.3 Normative Vulnerability

Mazzini suggests a kind of reflexive equilibrium to double check that a given normative decision is ok from the Law-of-God point of view, i.e., there must be an overlapping of individual conscience and universal consent. The language is, well, Mazzini's language:

> God has given you both the consent of your fellow-men, and your own conscience, even as two wings, wherewith to elevate yourselves towards Him. Why persist in cutting off one of them? Wherefore either isolate yourselves from, or absorb yourselves in, the world?[16]

One option is to isolate oneself from the "world", i.e., from a given set of shared beliefs, from an institutional *world*, from a normative horizon within which our arguments and decisions find their meaning. This means to rely exclusively on an individual, technical rationality, a means-end rationality shedding light on hard facts, whose functioning it is possible to describe. This is Mazzini's *egotism*. The other option is to absorb ourselves in the world: i.e., to identify fully and completely with a given normative horizon, giving up the possibility of criticizing it (in order either to legitimate it again, or to reform, edit, change, or substitute it with a more *advanced*, to use Mazzini's word, one). This is Mazzini's *tyranny*.

Mazzini is, however, aiming at something different. He needs to navigate that perilous equilibrium where a normative *world* is respected because it is valuable, and at the same time a condition of its value is to be inherently exposed to a principled critique:[17] the principles that allow such criticism are exclusively those already immanent in the institutional horizon of that given *world*, i.e., the overriding value of fighting and arguing against inequality and oppression.

There is always room for improvement, as it were, since "no man, no people, and no age may pretend to have discovered the whole of the Law".[18] It is not possible to reach a final conclusion, because this open structure makes sure that any given stage of development, any *world*, is exposed to principled critique.

The hint at this notion of universal humanity is important, since for Mazzini human beings, social animals after all, find the meaning of their existence within three circles: the family, the country, and humanity itself—which is the most important one from a normative point of view. God is responsible for the Law of Life of Humanity, which on the one side is all that matters, and on the other hand simply states that "solely through the medium of association" men are capable of "a progress to which none may assign a limit". The point, however, is that "[t]his is all we as yet know with regard to the Law of Humanity". These are the characteristics

[16]Mazzini (1862), p. 55.

[17]The idea that there are aspects of human flourishing that are valuable not so much despite their fragility, but because of it, was famously at the center of Nussbaum's reflection in Nussbaum (1986).

[18]Mazzini (1862), *The Duties of Man*, p. 62.

that "constitute human nature".[19] There is nothing else. No content. No resting place. God's law is to fight against inequalities and oppressions, whatever unforeseeable forms they may take, nested as they may be in institutions and norms. There is no dense anthropology, no substantial natural law.

It is a dirty job after all, because every equilibrium is provisional, and no human being can reach an Archimedean point outside the system. Principled critique is a joint venture of people who are creating a different set of beliefs: "It is of no avail to assert your own purity, even were true purity possible in isolation".[20]

Never does Mazzini mentions the afterlife, the fate of human beings beyond the veil of death; never does he mentions rites, prayer, theology, liturgy, eternity. "It is of import that human nature [. . .] may [. . .] realize still further the Design of God *on earth*".[21] In other words, in *The Duties of Men* God's role is to make sure that human beings do not need any special, peculiar, God, and that they simply keep fighting against inequalities and oppressions here on earth. And yes, "[o]ther and vaster duties will be revealed to us in the future".[22] Mazzini looks sometimes like an über-deist.

This means that inequalities and oppressions are somehow inherent in the human condition, and *this* seems to be a universal feature, a range quality, that makes it possible to speak of universal equality. The "first duties" are "towards Humanity", not toward country or family—differences no longer matter:

> Say not: *the language we speak is different.* Acts, tears, and martyrdom, are a language common to all men, and which all understand.[23]

In other words: equality is a key feature of human beings because they are all *vulnerable* (tears), and because they can all resist (acts) such a dire situation. This vulnerability is a normative, i.e., legal and political, vulnerability: martyrdom is not something that can be conjured up if the tears are shed because of a disease or a sudden loss—martyrdom implies a resistance to oppression and a public statement. In a nutshell: equality is predicated on normative vulnerability. It is not so much a value described once for all, it is a practice that is triggered "wheresoever fellow creature suffers, or the dignity of human nature is violated",[24] i.e., by a given kind of contingent vulnerability.

There is a back-and-forth itinerary to the fighting for a (more advanced) normative horizon (i.e., a given equality practice), from the underpinning notion of equality *per se*: the latter seems to exist because of the push implied by the principled critique inherent in the former, that however seems, in turn, to imply the former as a

[19]Mazzini (1862), *The Duties of Man*, pp. 66–67.

[20]Mazzini (1862), p. 69. This is again a vichian theme; see Vico (1990), XV, p. 80.

[21]Mazzini (1862), p. 73, italics mine.

[22]Mazzini (1862), p. 78.

[23]Mazzini (1862), p. 83.

[24]Mazzini (1862), p. 85.

condition of possibility. This means that *thought* and *action* are the same: Each is implied by the other.

8.3.1 Situated Vulnerabilities

This equality is possible because of the natural sociability of human beings, clearly endowed with a potential empathy for tears and sufferings of their fellows. This social impulse, however, plays a further role in *The Duties of Men*. Mazzini clearly states that God "divided Humanity into distinct groups or nuclei upon the face of earth, thus creating the germ of Nationalities".[25] Of course, this is Mazzini-the-Patriot aiming at the notion of *Patria-Nazione*, the necessary concept by which he could advocate the Unity of Italy as a nation. It is not meaningless, however, that from a theoretical point of view, he is bound to reach a more general notion of nuclei or groups.

Once again, the content of any association is simply equality: [t]here is no true association except among equals", there is "no true Country where the uniformity of Right is violated by [. . .] inequality".[26]

> God at the Summit; a people of equals at the base. Accept no other formula [. . .].[27]

God, however, is a concept empty of any possible substantial content, whose only function is to trigger equality practices; the equality at the base, on the other hand, is equally empty, because there are only equality practices, in the plural, in order to take care of contingent and situated forms of inequality—vulnerabilities that imply tears and sufferings.

The "pillars of the Nation", therefore, are not shared customs, mores, language, religion, traditions, ancestors, blood—those thick and dense, rich and juicy, features of a "primary equality". On the contrary "Education, labor, and the franchise, are the three main pillars of the Nation":[28] these are, as it were, features of "critical equality". Fighting for these three values was the equality practice called for by the situated vulnerability that was contingently relevant in the *world*, the normative horizon, that stood before Mazzini. Those were the inequalities mostly responsible for the tears and the sufferings of his fellow human beings in the Italian and European nineteenth century.

A specific group was under oppression, because of painful inequalities as far as education, labor, and franchise were concerned; a specific group was contingently

[25] Mazzini (1862), p. 87.

[26] Mazzini (1862), pp. 90–91. This will be the position challenged by Santi Romano—institutions do not seem to require equality. Interestingly, fascist thinkers like Giovanni Gentile tried to make a political use of Mazzini's thought: Levis Sullam (2015).

[27] Mazzini (1862), p. 92.

[28] Mazzini (1862), p. 94.

the victim/subject of a situated vulnerability that called for an equality practice: women. The following statement is already, in itself, an equality practice:

> Cancel from your minds every idea of superiority over Woman. You have none whatsoever.[29]

We can find disturbing the dangerous idealization of women as the "Angels" of the family, and even more the undisputable fact that Mazzini here, while advocating equality for women, is addressing exclusively an audience of men ("your minds [. . .] superiority over Woman"). It must be, however, acknowledged here that Mazzini, who must have read well his Vico, openly expresses the *normative inversion* which very often triggers the most heinous inequality practices and institutions. The rationale for unequal treatment is often that there is no basic equality to begin with. If subjects are not, from a basic point of view, equals, they cannot be treated as equals. According to the alternative itinerary we have outlined in Vico,[30] however, it is exactly a normative inequality practice (i.e., inequality-based institutions and norms) that do create basic inequality—the latter being the outcome of such a practice, not its rationale. Mazzini could not be clearer than that, and this alone makes a compelling argument for including *The Duties of Men* in a textbook on *Equality and Vulnerability*:

> Long prejudice, an inferior education, and a perennial legal inequality and injustice, have created that *apparent* intellectual inferiority which has been converted into an argument of continued oppression.
>
> But does not the history of every oppression teach us how the oppressor ever seeks his justification and support by appealing to a *fact* of his creation?.[31]

Situated vulnerabilities (within and because of a given narrative) are the outcome of inequality practices and institutions (punctual efficacy phenomena that claim their own legitimacy). There are analogies with the color line in Nineteenth Century America, *and with the Italian desire of independence*:

> The Slaveholders (sic) of America declare the black race radically inferior and incapable of education, and yet persecute those who seek to instruct them.
>
> For half a century the supporters of the reigning families have declared the Italians unfit for freedom, and meanwhile, by their laws, and by the brute force of hireling armies, they close every path through which we might overcome the obstacles to our improvement, did they really exist, as if tyranny could ever be a means of educating men for liberty.[32]

Equality is not just something that can be predicated of mere, "naked", unencumbered individuals. Situated individuals do matter: women, blacks—and Italians. Groups are valuable because of the complex interaction that links vulnerability

---

[29] Mazzini (1862), p. 99.

[30] See in this volume, *Paradoxes of Equality: Giambattista Vico.*

[31] Mazzini (1862), p. 99.

[32] Mazzini (1862), p. 100. Mazzini, a white man, is here choosing as partners women and blacks. There are dark pages in *The Duties of Man,* but this is not one of them.

and equality: on the one hand, there are groups, and individuals/members that are vulnerable because of that membership; on the other, groups are valuable precisely because they can trigger an equality practice which will edit, reform, improve, "advance", the general notion of equality.

> Suppose that a new and true principle, a new and rational development of the truths that have given vitality to the State, should be discovered by a few among its citizens. How shall they diffuse the knowledge of this principle except by association?
>
> Suppose that in consequence of scientific discovery, or of a new means of communication opened up between peoples and peoples, or from any other country, a new *interest* should arise among a certain number of the individuals composing the State. How shall they who first perceive this, make their way among the various interests of long standing, unless by uniting their efforts and their means? [...] The association of a daily increasing minority [...] is the method of the future.[33]

These minorities, these groups, are valuable—their very existence is a legitimizing factor of the larger society, because they constitute subaltern counterpublics[34] that ask for respect and recognition.

Dante, an author Mazzini had carefully studied, is quoted in a key passage of *The Duties of Men*: it is the old problem of the unity of all human beings under a single authority. "God is One. [...] Humanity is One. [...] Humanity exists; hence there must be a single aim for all men, a work to be achieved by all[35]" This quote is Mazzini quoting Dante: but now the oneness of humanity is simply a critical, not a substantial, concept: it simply means that "there cannot be [...] infallibility either in man or Powers", that "there is not, there cannot be, need of any interpreter between God and man, save Humanity".[36]

Nothing is left: because this notion of humanity is just the ever possible principled critique of a given institutional horizon. Critique, i.e., equality as a practice, *rectius* as practices against situated vulnerabilities, is what grants human beings their "humanity". The only common ground is this ever possible, ever necessary struggle over equality:

> True liberty cannot exist without equality, and equality can only exist among those who start from a common ground, a common principle, and a uniform consciousness and knowledge of duty.[37]

The common ground, the basic equality factor among human beings, is human vulnerability *and therefore* the consequent *principle*, the unsubstantial consciousness of a duty: the contingent motivating factor that triggers an equality practice.

The *Duties of Men* is an equality practice. It addressed specific inequalities. The Apostle of equality makes room for a special exception: one should heed the *genio*,

---

[33]Mazzini (1862), pp. 158–159.

[34]I am obviously making a very free use Nancy Fraser's expression in Fraser (1990).

[35]Mazzini (1862), p. 120.

[36]Mazzini (1862), p. 123.

[37]Mazzini (1862), p. 149.

the genius, of those men who are endowed with it. Genius entails a special authority: Gerolamo Cardano stated that he, like Socrates, had a genius, whose voice he could hear. Mazzini is suggesting that he himself has genius, and that his book is therefore a performative text that is going to change the meaning of equality.

References

Dal Lago E (2013) William Lloyd Garrison and Giuseppe Mazzini: abolition, democracy, and radical reform. Louisiana State University Press, Baton Rouge
Fraser N (1990) Rethinking the public sphere: a contribution to the critique of actually existing democracy. Soc Text 25–26:56–80
Levis Sullam S (2015) Giuseppe Mazzini and the origins of fascism. Palgrave Macmillan, New York
Mack Smith D (1996) Mazzini. Yale University Press, New Haven
Mathieu V (1989) Luci e ombre del giusnaturalismo. Giappichelli, Turin
Mazzini G [1860] (1862) The duties of man. Chapman & Hall, London
Mazzini G (2011) In: Sarti R, Mayper N (eds) Dear Kate. Lettere inedite di Giuseppe Mazzini a Katherine Hill, Angelo Bezzi e altri italiani a Londra (1841–1871). Rubbettino, Soveria Mannelli, (CZ)
Nussbaum M (1986) The fragility of goodness. Cambridge University Press, Cambridge
Recchia S, Urbinati N (eds) (2009) A cosmopolitanism of nations: Giuseppe Mazzini's writings on democracy, nation building, and international relations. Princeton University Press, Princeton
Urbinati N (2012) Mazzini and the making of the republican ideology. J Mod Ital Stud 17(2): 183–204
Vico G (1709) De nostri temporis studiorum ratione. English edition: Vico (1990) On the study methods of our time (trans. Gianturco E.) Cornell University Press, Ithaca
Viroli M (2008) L'Italia dei Doveri. Rizzoli, Milan

Chapter 9
Social Pluralism, Efficacy and Equality: Rethinking *The Legal Order* by Santi Romano

9.1 An Institutionalist Narrative

Santi Romano is a controversial figure in Italian jurisprudence. It cannot, and it should not, ever be forgotten that he was not just a member of the PNF, the National Fascist Party, and that he was not just appointed Chair of the Consiglio di Stato by Benito Mussolini himself, but that he was also member of the scientific board of a racist journal, *Il diritto razzista* (The Racist Law).[1]

His career was as brilliant as it could have been in those days: decorations, honors, memberships to the most important *Accademie*, lofty university tenures. The king appointed him a Senator of the kingdom; when this honor was definitely repealed, after World War II, because of his support for Mussolini, Romano had already died—he basically got away with that. There is no way to minimize, question, or contextualize these facts; there is nothing to object to these historical data.

Despite his many contributions in public and constitutional law, Romano is basically an *auctor libri unius*, the author of a single book (he published several):

[1]The very first paper is by the Editor-in-Chief, whose main title, duly reported on the Cover of the Journal and in the Index, is to be a *squadrista*, i.e., a member of the fascist action squads: "Il diritto razzista. Dottrina, Giurisprudenza, Legislazione Italiane e Straniere Sulla Famiglia e Sulla Razza. Diretta dallo squadrista Stefano M. Cutelli, Avvocato in Cassazione." The first name of the Scientific Board, Comitato Scientifico, is that of S.E. S. Romano, Presid. Consiglio di Stato. In his paper, *Ai lettori: Perché e come nasce Il diritto razzista e come è accolto* (1939-XVII, I, 1–2, pp. 1–8), Cutelli proudly quotes Santi Romano's reaction: "S.E. il prof. Santi Romano, Presidente del Consiglio di Stato, ha, ad esempio, scritto quanto segue: 'Mi pregio comunicarvi che accetto di buon grado di far parte del Comitato Scientifico del nuovo periodico Diritto Razzista, rivista di dottrina, diritto e giurisprudenza della razza, da voi così autorevolmente diretta'" (p. 5).

G. Zanetti, *Equality and Vulnerability in the Context of Italian Political Philosophy*, Studies in the History of Law and Justice 26,
https://doi.org/10.1007/978-3-031-35553-0_9

The Legal Order, a small volume that can still question the most widespread assumptions about law and order.[2]

First and foremost, Romano had a very different approach than Kelsen's. According to Kelsen legal systems were made of norms, and nothing else; the origin of a norm could only be another norm; at the top of the pyramid-like system there was a Fundamental Norm that had its origin half in itself and half in the logical need of the system. Romano was aware of Kelsen's doctrine, and the pure theory of law is mentioned in the very first footnote of his book.[3] There was going to be a controversy between the two scholars.

According to Romano, law is actually co-existent with social formations: there cannot be the former without the latter, and the other way around. Where there is a "society" of any kind there must be some kind of law; on the other hand, where there is any kind of law there must be a social formation of some kind. Norms can certainly be very important, but in order to be able to conceptualize them as legal norms, it is first necessary to have conceived law as the fundamental organization, structure and existential position of a society (Romano would have never used the word 'existential'), which is therefore constituted as a unity of some kind. Within this societal unity, and only within it, any legal relationship disciplined by the norm makes sense. Law is therefore first and foremost institution, which is why Romano's theory is known as (a form of) institutionalism.[4]

Romano does not believe that norms are "unimportant", he simply stresses that to see legal systems only *sub specie regulae*, from the point of view of the norms, can lead to oblivion of other and more fundamental aspects of the legal order. This means that there is an important theoretical layer in *The Legal Order* that is basically about the definition of "law", about that "something" (the *quid*) that bestows unity to the whole, and that challenges both the notion of a legal system as a "arithmetic sum" of norms (something Kelsen actually never said) and the idea that such a *quid* can somehow be hosted within a lofty, ozonic, ungraspable Fundamental Norm.

Another layer is some kind of primacy of public law over private law (Romano was a public law Professor): it was a mistake to use notions that were created within the latter to understand the former. And there can be no law for individuals per se: law must be understood on the background of a collective *self*, which is more than an aggregation of individual entities.

This is, however, not without severe consequences, because it leads to the notion that not just the State is institution, but any (structured, organized) social body qualifies; and that means that law is not an exclusive monopoly of the national State. Institutions are an effect of the social nature of human beings, and come in different flavors: they must have an identity, however, and they can have complex relationships one with another, because an institution, per se, does not need

---

[2]Romano [1918] (2018). See also Romano (2017) in the English translation by Mariano Croce (Routledge).

[3]See in this volume, *Dante Alighieri, Hans Kelsen, and the* Principium Unitatis.

[4]De Wilde (2018), pp. 12–24. See also Croce and Goldoni (2020).

autonomy. There are institutions within institutions. On the other hand, it is *not* law what, and only what, has no social organization.

This means that, from Santi Romano's point of view, it is perfectly pointless to try to determine the peculiar features of legal phenomena vs. religious or moral ones. Morality, religion, economy, the world of technical rules, and so on can always be absorbed in the legal world, each time one of these spheres is attracted within the efficacy radius of an institution.[5]

Romano, furthermore, tries hard to position himself in an Archimedean point outside the legal narrative, to enjoy a view from nowhere: from such a vantage point he can claim that it is not a norm that creates the legal order, and the origin of such an order is no law-structured process—but "as it has several times been stressed, a fact".[6]

This can be true, but it is not overly informative, because at the end of the day everything can be conceived as "a fact". We are close to a tautology: a bubble of efficacy of any kind is a fact, and when such a bubble creates its narrative, we can perceive legal phenomena. Legal phenomena do not exist per se, as facts independent from any narrative they may radiate: mere "blind" facts could not be labeled as legal under such circumstances. When a narrative of some kind sheds some non-neutral light on some facts, leaving other facts in the dark, those (or some) facts appear as legal phenomena. We seem to have a Santi Romano creating, expounding, reinforcing a given (institutionalist) narrative, and at the same time a Santi Romano watching the process engaged by his twin. Efficacy is both the name of a fact (something happens) and the label-giving process of a narrative (acknowledgment of that "something happens" as a normative horizon of some kind).

9.2 The Legal Order

While a system of valid legal norms presents itself as unified, structured, and consistent, efficacy per se does not require this much. The narrative by which efficacy facts are perceived as legal phenomena, on the other hand, projects on those facts qualities that define the identity of the system—such a projection has little to do with an objective description of inherent features predicated of a given reality, there is no mirror-like correspondence granted by any reassuring metaphysical assumption.

[5]Romano (2017), pp. 21–22. Mariano Croce points out to me that Romano believes that "organization" is a basic phenomenon; law allows us to describe it in a specific way - other sciences describe it otherwise. Romano's approach seems to imply a radical perspectivism.

[6]Romano (2017), p. 24. There are different positions on this point. According to Croce, Romano's law is not a mere fact, but knowledge that grows around a practice (knowledge of those normative elements that provide "persistence" to a given social group). In a nutshell, law consists of practice, and of knowledge of that practice.

As a matter of fact, any narrative necessarily selects some facts as normatively relevant, and obscures other. The resulting normative world may well need to identify itself as a unity, but the reality behind the narrative needs not to be a unity at all; it would be reasonable to suppose that it is precisely the lack of unity of efficacy phenomena that requires the "bracketing away" operation implied by a given legal narrative. This also means that the legal order, any legal order, is by definition a *limited* legal order.[7]

Santi Romano, nevertheless, does not agree with Jellinek, and there are some lines in *The Legal Order* that are directly written against him (although he does acknowledge him among the *autorevoli*).[8] There is, however, an interesting ambiguity here. First Romano claims that the theory of State self-limitation cannot be accepted in the wider wording that his author adopted. Next, he proceeds to offer a formula that seems much wider that the one submitted by Jellinek. He claims that even if we grant that the State limits itself when it determines its own legal order, it remains true that it could not be limitless even before such an act, because the State is a legal order and is an institution in itself, from the beginning: self-limitation can therefore be nothing more than a *further* (*ulteriore*) limitation.

The notion of a State that pre-exists its constitution is a puzzling one, if one does not consider its possible religious roots. Jellinek and Romano, however, are struggling with the same problem. Something happens, and when we can perceive this something it is already somehow shaped and therefore limited; what is genetically prior to the "something" is beyond our perception power, and can therefore be either labeled with a most generic term (*facts*) or identified with an entity that defies any empirical, sensorial or historical, evidence, and must be merely presupposed in order to allow normative rationality to flourish (the "impossible" State without Constitution that has *not yet* limited itself).

Romano himself seems almost to somehow smell the religious undertones of Jellinek's doctrine:[9] the legislator, he says, is not the creator of the law, in the full and absolute meaning of the word, i.e., the first creator. And finally, he rushes to touch another of Jellinek's points: the legislator is not endowed with the power to fully, completely annihilate law, because in order to utterly destroy law he should also sanction the end of the State.

It is possible to appreciate here the subtlety of the problem: the narrative that makes efficacy phenomena normatively relevant, and therefore existing from the point of view of the subject, is anything permanent or stable. As long as efficacy phenomena are perceived as such, however, they enjoy that relative autonomy that makes them impervious to any destruction: which is why all legal orders must one day or the other end in ashes, and at the same time they must conceptualize themselves as eternal and indestructible—stars and stripes forever,[10] *Alme sol*

[7] See in this volume, *The Limits of Law and Arturo Carlo Jemolo's Islands* (*passim*).

[8] Romano (2017), para 22, p. 42.

[9] See in this volume, *The Limits of Law and ArturCarlo Jemolo's Islands*, 11.1.

[10] Bierley (2001).

[. . .] possis tu nihil urbe Roma, visere maius.[11] Any legal order is eternal in the moment of its perception, but on the other hand it does not seem to have any other existence than this perception-based, punctual, one. Behind the narrative there are phenomena which are not truly available to the subject perception: they become available only under the strictures of a given selective narrative.

Romano must have sensed the problem. At the very end of the First Chapter of *The Legal Order*, therefore in a rhetorically strategic position, where he is taking stock of his grand proposal, Romano clarifies his contribution. First, he says, quite modestly for someone who has just sharply criticized some of the most outstanding jurisprudence scholars of his time, that he has merely set some borders to the notion of law, the very same borders that the "tradition" has always factually (*materialmente*) recognized, although without providing a precise theoretical definition (and that is Romano's contribution from his own point of view). This sounds like a *rappel a l'ordre* after the normativistic infatuation of jurisprudence's latest fashion trends.

After this seemingly modest remark, Romano stresses how his proposal makes no use of natural law. He fashions himself, as a matter of fact, as an uber-positivist:

> The concept of institution, in which I found, or, better, with which I identified that of the legal order, is the most positive concept that a legal theory can take as its basis. The institution is not a rational requirement (*esigenza della ragione*), an abstract principle, an ideal *quid*– it is a real, effective entity.[12]

There is no doubt that an institution, and any legal order, is an entity that is real, in the sense that we can speak of it in a reasonable way, an entity that falls under our intellectual perception as something effective—it is a bubble of shaped efficacy, and therefore it "works" from the point of view of the subject. Unfortunately for Romano, an institution needs to be intellectually perceived in order to exist, because it is a more or less arbitrary selection of efficacy phenomena that nevertheless do not pre-exist to the selecting narrative. The naïf social metaphysics presupposed by Romano reveals itself in the Kantian lexicon he adopts as an exorcism (rational requirement, need of reason, *Bedürfnis der Vernunft*). With a remarkable intellectual honesty, he goes on:

> On the other hand, I heeded this entity not from the point of view of the material forces that produce and sustain it, nor in relation to the environment where it develops and lives as a phenomenon intertwined with others, nor with regard to cause-effect relationships that affect it, and therefore, not sociologically, but in itself and for itself, inasmuch as it results from a legal order or, better, it is a system of law. Naturally, I had to go further up to the ultimate regions, where one can breathe the legal atmosphere, but I never surpassed it.[13]

In other words, Romano did choose, as a methodology, the legal system and its narrative as a starting point. His notion of institution, therefore, is still the product of a methodological wishful thinking, that tries to bestow a stable "reality" on mere

[11] Horace (Quintus Horatius Flaccus), *Carmen Saeculare*, 9–12.

[12] Romano (2017), p. 46.

[13] Romano (2017), para 24, pp. 46–47. I guess "reasons" is a typo.

efficacy phenomena which are conceptualized this way only because of a selective narrative. Romano is wonderfully aware that institutions can be different even within the same *genus*, and it is quite remarkable how he stresses the differences between different historical notions/institutions of family. He nevertheless had to buy into the same narrative he could glimpse, and therefore grant his pet notion, institution, a "positive" reality, the status of a "fact", a quality that was just the necessary reflection of the very narrative that allowed him to perceive it as such. In a way, he went as far as he could.

9.3 The Risks of Selective Equality

There is a dark spot though, in this end of Chapter One. Santi Romano, quite *en passant*, touches the problem of equality. The fascist author stresses that there is no necessary equality in an institution, in a given legal order. It is not true, according to Romano, that "di fronte al diritto obiettivo tutti i subbietti siano da considerarsi eguali", that all subjects are to be seen as equals before the law. As a matter of fact, both the supremacy of the State and the position of the subjects fall within the radius of the legal order and are therefore determined by the legal order. This is an authoritarian threat: in the institution of the State, in the legal order, inequalities and discriminations can and do exist.

This notion can be used as a critical scrutiny device: with problems of equality and vulnerability in mind, it is possible to warn that even those legal systems that claim to cherish equality could (or must) hide some dark areas of invisible discrimination. Such an inequality can be invisible precisely because institutions can and do have a constitutive blind spot: they arise selectively validating some efficacy phenomena, they are known exclusively through a narrative within which it is sometimes possible to reach for equality. Such an equality is necessarily selective and therefore partial: sometimes, however, "it must" present itself as universal because of the logical strictures determined by that given narrative.

Political rights equality means, for example, universal suffrage—which in England was however not understood as including women before the women's suffrage movement. In Italy universal suffrage inclusive of women dates from 1945; the right to vote was exercised by women for the first time during the 1946 referendum.

It is not just that a narrative of equality does not necessarily imply universal equality: it can as well hide and cloud stark inequalities and severe discriminations. This means that equality claims imply a resistance, because the vulnerable groups are bracketed away in the universal narrative of equality that bestows on a given legal system both identity and legitimacy at the same time.

If Romano is right, this simply proves that it is always sensible to be suspicious, and the burden of proof remains with the legal system itself—not on the subject or the vulnerable group ("when in doubt, be inclusive").

The second chapter of *The Legal System* is about the pluralism of legal systems. The usual positivistic approach would see a plurality of legal systems only because there is a plurality of states. Law is only state law (*and* international law). Santi Romano, on the other hand, believes that in the Middle Age it was crystal clear that there can exist more than one legal system, more than one kind of law. The modern State claims to have the right to monopolize law production. There is little doubt that such is the legitimizing narrative of the national modern state. According to Romano, however, state law is just a species of the genus law.

The first *second* legal system that enters the stage is of course the Church. To reduce the Church order, the Church institution, the Church (canon) law, to State order, simply means to misrecognize it, and to annihilate, it (*disconoscerlo e annientarlo*[14]). There is little doubt that part and parcel of Church Law is a narrative of autonomy: according to Church Law, Church Law is not derivative or secondary, it does not rely on the State as the ultimate source of its existence, identity, and legitimacy. Dante's Cesar, according to Kelsen, should have not, however, recognized Peter as his superior.

State Law and Church Law are two normative legal worlds, each of which can materially affect (*materialmente influire*) the other, that from a legal point of view can and do remain distinct and autonomous one from another.[15] As a matter of fact, each normative system can and often did conceptualize itself as primary and overriding, the source of any other possible normative order, a problem well known to Dante.

Romano is, however, adamant: organized illegal institutions are institutions, and therefore legal orders, as well. Mafia, or better *Cosa nostra* is quite a structured and organized institution, with its own set of rules and an extremely effective sanctions system. In the well-known § 30 of *The Legal Order* is clearly written that it is immaterial that from the State legal order point of view *Cosa nostra* is illegal. Its efficacy *sarà quella che sarà*, "will be what it will be"—which is quite an accurate formula for any efficacy array of phenomena. Interestingly, Romano adds that when the State will be strong the mafia organization will be weak, and the other way around: the efficacy of an institution has to do with an interplay of expansion and compression because of the existence of other efficacy institutions, even if there is no acknowledgment of other systems as legal systems.

Romano granted the lofty status of legal order to *any* normative structured reality, i.e., institutions. He certainly did not bestow that lofty status to unstructured comprehensive groups—but hasn't any given comprehensive group to be, even minimally, structured?

The scope of his notion of pluralism, however, should be appreciated. Comprehensive groups can certainly be unstructured, but they can develop and share a legal narrative that appropriates the narrative of another, structured, entity. They can be

---

[14]Romano (2017), p. 55. *In utroque iure* meant for several centuries (to have a degree) in both canon and civil law.

[15]Romano (2017), p. 58.

acknowledged with their own narrative within the legal system of the *larger society*, i.e., within State law. They are therefore not necessarily immaterial from a legal point of view.

Comprehensive groups are situated groups: they can be extremely different one from another—differences more radical than those between Church and mafia. Membership within a given comprehensive group can create forms of situated vulnerability, a peculiar position of disadvantage in the interaction with other groups and institutions *and* within a given State legal order, since—as Santi Romano pointed out—there is no equality among subjects necessarily implied in this peculiar Legal Order.

This means that there will always be vulnerability problems, and that equality is not good health, but a—complex, each time different—therapy.

References

Bierley P-E (2001) John Philip Sousa: American Phenomenon. Warner Bros. Publications, Miami

Croce M, Goldoni M (2020) The legacy of pluralism: the continental jurisprudence of Santi Romano, Carl Schmitt, and Costantino Mortati. Standford University Press, Redwood City

De Wilde M (2018) The dark side of institutionalism: Carl Schmitt reading Santi Romano. J Ethics Glob Polit 11(2):12–24

Romano S [1918] L'ordinamento giuridico. Quodlibet, Macerata. English edition: Romano (2017) The legal order (trans: Croce M). Routledge, New York

Romano S (2017) The legal order. Routledge, New York

Chapter 10
From Emilio Salgari to Cesare Lombroso – Racism and Law in Italy: Situated Vulnerability

10.1 Books for Italian Children

Emilio Salgari is a well-known Italian author of books for children. Italians of my generation grew up reading the adventures of Sandokan, the Malaysian Tiger, a most brave pirate. He was merciless but with his own honor code, always faithful to his word and invincible in a duel.

The writer described in painstaking detail the landscape and the vegetation of faraway countries he had never visited (he was an avid reader of geography texts in the Turin public library). He also falsely pretended to have been Commander in Chief on a boat, and for this boasting lie, he had to eventually engage in a real duel. Salgari did not end up well: he took his own life, disemboweling himself in a horrific way, using a razor. He had a very unhappy life, that included a suicide of his father, a wife hospitalized in a psychiatric institution, no true social recognition at all, and no financial stability. All of his children met a tragic death as well.

One of his most famous books is *The Pirates of Malaysia*, published in 1896. The main characters of this fiction are three proud warriors, who are going to become great friends. The leader is the above mentioned Sandokan, originally a Borneo nobleman,[1] with his loyal sidekick, Yanez de Gomera, a pureblood Portuguese, as he imagines himself. The third friend is a handsome Bengali, Tremal-Naik, approximately thirty years old, with an *olivastra* (fairly dark) skin.[2]

In one or the other books of Salgari's "Pirates Series", each of the three main characters is duly engaged in a romantic affair, or a passionate love story. Sandokan falls for the daughter of an enemy, Marianne Guillonk, nicknamed the Pearl of Labuan. Yanez is in love with Surama, a lady from the Assam region. In *The Pirates of Malaysia* the main love story is that between Tremal-Naik and Ada Corisant, a

[1] Salgari [1896] (1967), p. 52. See also Salgari (2006) in the English translation by Nico Lorenzutti.
[2] Salgari [1887] (1966), p. 9. See also Salgari (2009) in the English translation by Nico Lorenzutti.

G. Zanetti, *Equality and Vulnerability in the Context of Italian Political Philosophy*, Studies in the History of Law and Justice 26,
https://doi.org/10.1007/978-3-031-35553-0_10

young English lady abducted by the *thugs*. They are worshippers of the Hindu Kali deity, who strangle their enemies or victims, led by the evil "Tiger of India", Suyodhana.

While it is mercifully not necessary to get into the details of the plot, it should be remarked that none of the main characters falls in love with a partner of his or her own ethnicity. Sandokan and Tremal-naik are Asian, men of color anyway, and they both marry an English lady (Marianne and Ada are cousins, by the way). Yanez, the only caucasian member of the trio, is engaged with Surama. It is also worth remarking that even the cruel Suyodhana, the leader of the Kali worshippers who dwell in dark, secret underground tunnels of India, did conceive a son, Tenent Moreland, with an English lady. In other terms, it looks like Salgari's main characters usually fall for partners who do not belong to their same "racial" group.

Since Ada Corisant is 15 years old,[3] on the other hand, her relationship with Tremal-Naik would have been statutory rape in several countries—and those were books that loving mothers would give to their 8, 9 years old children so that they could learn to love reading. It is quite certain that such an age gap would mean big trouble for any contemporary writer who would dare to describe a love relationship like that in a glamorous, positive way.

This may help, however, to better understand the lack of any word, in Italian, that translates 'miscegenation'. There is, actually, no word for it. The French mésalliance means a marriage between partners who belong to different social classes—a different kind of prejudice, although they both forbid some kind of union (mésalliance was forbidden by custom, not by law).

Unfortunately, this does not mean at all that Italians never had a racism problem at home. Italians did have infamous racial laws during the Fascist period, well after Salgari's death. Salgari's books, furthermore, are littered with obscene, unacceptable racist expressions—while the Dayak people seem to have courage and audacity in their blood, the Chinese are often described with unacceptable derogatory words—quite a disgusting attitude that makes reading those books a very unpleasant experience. The only reason to recall them now, is to conjure up a cultural background where the "race" problems took an extremely specific, and still horrific, shape.

In Salgari, races are often mentioned. No Italian could find anything strange in the famous exchange at the very beginning of *The Pirates of Malaysia*, when Yanez spares the life of a young brave warrior of color, Kammamuri, who proudly asks him why a pirate is showing him mercy[4]:

– "Why are you not killing me?"
– "Well, to begin with, because you are not white".
– "Do you hate white men?"
– "Yes".
– "But aren't you ..."

[3] Salgari (1967), p. 26.

[4] Salgari (1967), p. 24.

– "Dammit, of course, pureblood Portuguese".
– "But then . . ."
– "Let us not talk about this".

The notion of a white man whose loyalty was with the brave folks of faraway Asia and their traditional values was something that Salgari could take for granted as perfectly acceptable and appropriate for Italian children of the year 1896.

There is, however, a "race" that does not, or does not often, get mentioned in his books—the Jewish race. This was not by chance: prejudice against Jewish people had a long history in the Peninsula, mostly on religious grounds, and the persecution it triggered could be most cruel.

10.2 Lombroso and Racism

During the fascist years, Italian racism took its peculiar, ambiguous shape. It is well known that Mussolini did not start as an open racist. In an early speech, he spoke dismissively of racist doctrines. One of his mistresses (for almost twenty years), for example, was Jewish, Margherita Sarfatti: one of the most learned women of her age, received by Eleanor Roosevelt with the kind of honors usually reserved for a first lady. Needless to say, everything changed when her beloved *Dux*, the title of Mussolini's biography she authored,[5] translated in several languages (including Turkish and Japanese), became an ally of Nazi Germany and officially embraced racism, something that prompted her to smartly leave the country. Her unlucky sister Nella was deported to the Auschwitz concentration camp in Poland, where she died with her husband.

The American physician Samuel A. Cartwright claimed that black slaves suffered from a psychiatric disease, so called drapetomania, the compulsive desire to escape from their masters (an illness unknown among white people), and that freed slaves were more susceptible to psychic unbalance than those who would live in servitude.[6] In Italy Cesare Lombroso, a Sephardim Jewish scholar, tried to establish a connection between some anatomic features and the impulse to perform criminal act. A Lombrosian explanation of a position *a là* Cartwright is given by Leonardo Di Caprio in *Django Unchained* by Quentin Tarantino[7]: blacks are prone to servitude because of some anatomic details of their skull. It does not really matter if the stigma of inferiority revolves around the impulse to seek freedom or the lack of it: the essential part is that there is an anatomic explanation for that stigma.

Lombroso was a positivistic scholar, he identified himself as a scientist, and was an atheist; he, by the way, was fascinated by Gerolamo Cardano, a human being

[5] Sarfatti (1926). See Urso (2003).

[6] Cartwright (1851), pp. 691–715 and pp. 707–709. See Hunt (1855), pp. 438–442.

[7] Quentin Tarantino, *Django Unchained*, 2012, starring Jamie Foxx, Christoph Waltz, Leonardo Di Caprio, Kerry Washington and Samuel L. Jackson.

where genius and psychiatric condition would blend.[8] His daughter Paola (a writer and an anthropologist herself) married the physician Mario Carrara, one of the Twelve Italian University Professors who dared to defy Fascism by not taking the required loyalty oath (for which they were all fired).[9] In the last period of his life, however, Lombroso took seriously Eusapia Palladino, a medium who was able to make him believe in spiritism.

Both a lawyer and a physician, Lombroso played a role in shaping the fears and the political goals of an Italian bourgeoisie; its need of law and order, and its aversion to diversity and minorities—something perceived as linked with chaos and lack of stability. It is possible to give an explanation for criminal acts, and sociopathic behaviors. It has to do with an anatomic feature, with biology. The urge to explain, to *erklären*, everything, with an "experimental" attitude, took eventually Lombroso to believe in mediums and spiritism.

Fascist racists, however, loathed Lombroso. Giuseppe Maggiore identified Lombroso, together with Freud and Marx, as a creator of the "materialistic Jewish culture of the Nineteenth century". Fascist authorities took aim at the Italian streets that were named after the Jewish Scientist.[10]

It does not, therefore, come as a surprise that Lombroso is still today a source of controversy. He had created a personal museum, that later became the Lombroso Museum in Turin. Although it is, from some points of view, a museum devoted mostly to debunked (and potentially dangerous) theories, it is an interesting proof of the way people of science would think in the Nineteenth Century.[11]

There is still the skull of the *brigante* Villella, the south Italian man whose autopsy had shown those signs that Lombroso thought could be the symptom of a criminal tendency. Some populist politicians required the return of the abducted skull, in order to give it a proper burial, after the outrageous defilement. The original plan included several memorial religious services on the road that would rightfully bring back Villella's rests to the very land where they belong.

There is a complexity to be appreciated in this tale. A major expression of situated vulnerability has been, and still is, in Italy, crystallized around the notion of "race". There is an interesting tension between the positivistic narrative of an objective knowledge (that can give rise to an oxymoric "scientific racism") and the fully arbitrary, ascriptive status of "race"- related statements.

Emilio Salgari seems to produce full-fledged racist statements: in his books some "races" are clearly seen as physically and morally superior than others. Yet white men and women are not, as one could expect, conceptualized as superior or purer

---

[8]Bellini (1947), p. 303. This book was published in a *Collana di studi di storia della medicina*. Important contributions by Mariacarla Gadebusch Bondio: see Bondio (2013), pp. 41–57. Cp. Lombroso (1855), Lombroso (1856), Lombroso (1857a), Lombroso (1857b), Lombroso (1857c), Lombroso (1864), Lombroso (1877).

[9]Goetz (1993). It is the Italian translation, by Loredana Melissari, of Goetz (1993).

[10]Montaldo (2012), pp. 137–146.

[11]Montaldo (2013), pp. 98–112.

than their partners. Sandokan, the man of color, is the leader: white Yanez is the sidekick. This is still an inarticulate prejudice, that does not seem to be directly related to a Lombrosian attitude.

10.3 Italian Racisms

Lombroso's thought, on the other hand, could fuel racist trains of thought, but he was targeted by card-carrying Italian racists on the infamous pages of the *La difesa della razza* journal (*The Defense of the Race*). Finally, the Lombroso Museum in Turin, and the figure of Lombroso himself, is now targeted by populist politicians, who charge him with the crime of racism; they ask (as racist Fascists did) to change the titles of those streets and squares that were named after him.

One of the most important Italian fascist "race"-theorists was Julius Evola.[12] While there is nothing to learn from his abominable doctrine, it can be important to see how the racist mind works when they try to take up the shape of a rational argument. It is interesting, for instance, to see that Italian racists can be in sharp disagreement with each other, and that often the epistemic grounds on which they build their racist positions are utterly incompatible.

Giorgio Almirante was a well-known politician during the Sixties, who graduated with a dissertation on Dante's *Fortuna* in the Eighteenth Century with Vittorio Rossi as a tutor, and who died at the end of the Eighties. He had been a full-fledged fascist and, after being rescued by German soldiers, had an official position in that Repubblica di Salò run by Mussolini. He was also, during the fascist *Ventennio*, a real racist. He advocated a blood and flesh racism, a racism ground on biology. To stress the role played by culture and spiritual factors, he thought, could have helped the clever Jewish people to claim some kind of conversion, to picture themselves as more Italians than Italian. His opponent was Julius Evola, who had quite a different view about racism. According to Evola, race had to do with souls more than with bodies, and with esoteric, ancestral factors. Almirante would call Evola and the like the foodies *(buongustai)* of racism—unable to appreciate the plebeian and yet robust flavor of a muscular racism based on blood. It must be remarked, however, that Evola's approach was not a softer one, and that his convoluted arguments were supported by photographs of members of the different racial groups. The idea that "race" is something eminently *visible*, that one can grasp *ictu oculi,* quickly *in the blinking of an eye*, is always there. The journal, "*The Defense of the Race*", had many illustrations, almost all of them extremely offensive and literally horrific.[13]

Italian racists, on the other hand, also tried hard to create a notion of a Roman-Aryan race, an almost desperate enterprise given the genetic diversity of the Italian

[12]Evola (1941).

[13]Valentina Pisanty received the original issues of *La difesa della razza* from Umberto Eco. Using these materials, she edited a most useful reader. See Pisanty (2006).

population. They had a little problem with the Etruscans because they did not even seem to be Indo-European. Sometimes they would deem them as an inferior group, nevertheless unable to stain and contaminate the Italian blood, and sometimes they would extoll the nobility of that aristocratic, brave people, a worthy contribution to the noble Italian race.

As a general rule, when Mussolini had the political need to cut some political slack for himself, to assume a stance of autonomy, he would lean to the Roman-Aryan racism, but when he needed to strengthen his alliance with Germany, he would embrace a more robust form of racism of the flesh-and-blood kind—which is what happened with the Racial Laws of 1938, when 50,000 Italians found themselves, quite suddenly, banned from civil society.

It is critical to understand that Italian racism tried to picture itself as based on science, or empirical evidence and that it was at the same time the most arbitrary, artificial, ideological position one could think. It is interesting, for example, to study the *fortuna* of the fabricated, notorious booklet, The *Protocols of the Elders of Zion*,[14] describing the Jewish plan for global domination. It was first published in Russia in 1903. An Italian translation, however, was published, edited by Giovanni Preziosi, only in 1921, the same year when the London *Times* exposed it as a fraud.[15] A new edition in 1937, i.e, after Mussolini had openly embraced racism, got a much higher attention, and three other editions followed suit. In the 1938 fifth edition, there is an Introduction by Evola himself, who was of course well aware that the *Protocols* had been exposed as fraudulent.[16] The racist scholar downplayed the problem stating that the issue was not if the Protocols were *authentic* (*autentici*), but if they were truthful (*veridici*). This could still be a motto for conspiracy theorists.

10.4 Arguments and Motivations

Reasonable arguments do not necessarily impact a motivation horizon that can be built on emotions. It is not just that the first Italian edition of the *Protocols* was published exactly when it had become apparent that they were the product of a forgery, but that a racist intellectual like Julius Evola had to delve into such subtle, desperate, hypocritical distinctions, in the vain attempt to spare himself the shame that he so abundantly deserved. There could be here an echo of his research in the Asian philosophy, since the Mahayana understanding of the later *sutras* tend to dismiss the authenticity problem. Even a spurious *sutra* can include a verse that is true Buddha Dharma, and in that case that verse is to be deemed both truthful and authentic. After the end of the regime, Evola kept harping on the same cords,

---

[14] Bronner (2003).

[15] Graves (1921). The title of the first article was: *A Literary Forgery*.

[16] Evola (1938).

although in much softer and careful tones, while Almirante rejected his former racism (he stressed the role played by both his young age and the historical context).

The *Manifesto of Italian Racists* signed by ten individuals who deemed themselves scientists (and published in the very first issue of the journal "The Defense of the Race", 1938), is an extremely interesting document. Its first points sound like scientific statements: "Human races do exist". According to the signatories, races mirror a material, phenomenal reality, that we can perceive with our senses. The notion of race is purely biological. A pure Italian race does exist. From point seven on, descriptive statements are replaced by a prescriptive stance: "7. It is time that Italians frankly proclaim themselves to be racists". "10. European characters of Italians should no way be altered". Before this last one, the point 9 ominously go back to an apparently descriptive statement: "Jewish people do not belong to the Italian race". The *Manifesto* tries to will into existence an institutional *world* where Jewish people can be victimized by "legitimate" law. It is a *world* that hosts, and revolve around, a most extreme kind of group vulnerability. Again, it is not that since these racists believed that Jewish people were different, they wanted to "discriminate" them. True as this may be, it still half of the tale. The other side was: since they wanted to discriminate them, they tried to will into existence a *world* where Jewish people *are* different—shaping beliefs and emotions, to begin with.

On the one hand, emphasis is on the senses—especially the sight, you can see the differences, they are visible. On the other hand, sight has a constitutive power, it helps to create these "races", with a power that is not just perception of an "outside" objective reality, but an active, aggressive, Medusa-like look, a killing glance that petrifies human beings in an ascriptive category. This active power is revealed in the arbitrary way it works, like a weapon one can aim against some subjects rather than against others: Germans were deemed as similar to Italians, French were not deemed as such—interesting problems were created by the preferential treatment these neutral scientists had to reserve to their Asian allies in the RoBerTo (Roma, Berlin, Tokio) axis, the Japanese.[17] Efficacy phenomena do radiate a narrative of some kind, but consistency is not a requirement, except for the late coming learned scholar who must try to square the circle.

There was a difference in the stereotypes created for the Jewish people and for the black Africans. The latter were pictured like childish, simple, not too smart men and women, who could be civilized by the Italians—this was obviously functional to the Italian colonial adventure in Africa. Jewish people were described with much darker colors: sly, clever, and greedy. This was the first step toward the carefully hued hate that would have murdered so many Italians of Jewish heritage.

The racial laws signed by the Italian King forbade, of course, any marriage between Jewish people and "Italians". Italian Soldiers would often temporarily "marry" a young black woman while fighting in African "colonies" (the so called *madamato*). A law was eventually passed to forbid this practice. Future journalist and writer Indro Montanelli, a leading figure in the field and much respected by

[17] Zanetti (2012), pp. 267–278; Zanetti (2020).

political adversaries as well, made use of such an institution, and "married" a young black girl only twelve years old—younger than Ada Corisant. Confronted by a black activist in the seventies during a tv program, he balked and tried to defend himself, claiming that customs in Africa were different. [18] The black woman replied that she was from Abyssinia, and that there was and there is no difference. Italians forgot this exchange, that took place when TVs were in black and white only, but it resurfaced during the Black Lives Matter activism. The statue of Indro Montanelli in Milan was defaced with red paint. Right wing politicians were outraged.

The tale of this cluster of Italian racism sheds light on the distinction between the horizon of arguments and the horizon of motivations. We usually pay attention to rational arguments, and a philosophical etiquette rule (almost two and half millennia old[19]) is never to mention the motivation horizon to refute a thesis: one must fight fire with fire, argument with argument. Still, motivational factors are intertwined with rational arguments in a complex way: it is extremely difficult to extricate and disentangle an argument from the contingent motivational horizon where it flourishes. Here we see a spiral of arguments twisting and stretching themselves under the pressure of relatively fluid motivational factors. The arguments per se would be facetious had they not been tragic: they were not so much aimed to justify, or to rationalize, as to create and reinforce those motivational factors. It did work.

Finally, this is a case of *situated vulnerability*: Jewish and African people are not vulnerable per se, because of some biological or spiritual and ancestral array of factors, but they are made vulnerable under a narrative that creates a motivational horizon where legal and political violence against them, shaped by the perceptive and semantic violence inherent in such a narrative, morphs into efficacy phenomena (that in turn need to radiate arguments that sometimes can achieve some kind of autonomy from the contingent context that made them appear in the first place).

Equality as a praxis is any practice that reacts to such pressure: the creation of effective counterarguments, the exposure of the motivational factors, the creation of an alternative motivational horizon through protest and direct political action.

References

Bellini A (1947) Gerolamo Cardano e il suo tempo. Ulrico Hoepli, Milan

Bronner S-E (2003) A Rumor About the Jews: Reflections on Antisemitism and the Protocols of the Learned Elders of Zion. Oxford University Press, Oxford

Cartwright S-A (1851) Report on the diseases and physical peculiarities of the negro race. New Orleans Med Surg J:691–715

Evola J (1938) I "protocolli" dei "savi anziani" di Sion. Trans: Preziosi G. La Vita italiana, Rome. (With an Essay by Julius Evola)

[18] *Montanelli e la moglie dodicenne* on YouTube. https://www.youtube.com/watch?v=PYgSwluzYxs. The Feminist activist was Elvira Banotti.

[19] Plato, *Gorg.*, 471d-e; *Resp.* 349a.

Evola J (1941) Sintesi di dottrina della razza. Hoepli, Milan
Gadebusch Bondio M (2013) La creatività di Cardano e la psichiatrizzazione del genio nell'Ottocento/ Cardanos Kreativität und die Psychiatrisierung des Genies im 19. Jh. In Ott C and Pfisterer U, Die biologie der Kreativität. Der menschliche Körper alskünstlerisches Reflexionesmedium von der Renaissance bis in die Gegenwart, Zürich, Berlin, pp 41–57
Goetz H (1993) Der Freie Geist und seine Widersacher. Haag + Herchen, Frankfurt a.M. Italian Edition: Goetz (2000) Il giuramento rifiutato. I docenti universitari e il regime fascista (trans: Melissari L). La Nuova Italia, Milan
Graves P (1921) "Jewish World Plot". An Exposure. The Source of the Protocols. Truth at Last. The Times. August 16–18
Hunt S-B (1855) Dr. Cartwright on 'Drapetomania'. Buffalo Med J: 438–442
Lombroso C (1855) Su la pazzia di Cardano – del signor Cesare Lombroso. Gazzetta medica italiana - Lombardia. Appendice psichiatrica, 40: s. III, VI, 34–45
Lombroso C (1856) Su la pazzia di Cardano – del signor Cesare Lombroso. Gazzetta medica italiana – Lombardia. Appendice psichiatrica 48: s. IV, I, 437–440
Lombroso C (1857a) Su la pazzia di Cardano – del signor Cesare Lombroso. Gazzetta medica italiana – Lombardia. Appendice psichiatrica 5:s. IV
Lombroso C (1857b) Su la pazzia di Cardano – del signor Cesare Lombroso. Gazzetta medica italiana – Lombardia. Appendice psichiatrica 5: II, 33–35
Lombroso C (1857c) Su la pazzia di Cardano – del signor Cesare Lombroso. Gazzetta medica italiana – Lombardia. Appendice psichiatrica 14: s. IV, II, 109–111
Lombroso C (1864) Genio e follia. Prelezione di corsi di Antropologia e Clinica psichiatrica presso l'Università di Pavia. Giuseppe Chiusi, Milan
Lombroso C (1877) Genio e follia. Hoepli, Milan
Montaldo S (2012) The skull, the mayor, the engineer, the judge and the comedian. An Italian museum feuilleton. Museologia Scientifica 6(1–2):137–146
Montaldo S (2013) The Lombroso Museum from its origins to the present day. In Knepper P et Ystehede P - J (eds) The Cesare Lombroso handbook. Routledge, New York
Pisanty V (2006) La difesa della razza. Antologia 1938–1943. Bompiani, Milan
Salgari (2006) The Pirates of Malaysia. Trans: Lorenzutti N. Roh Press
Salgari (2009) The Mistery of the Black Jungle. Trans: Lorenzutti N. Roh Press
Salgari E (1887) I misteri della giungla nera. Vallardi, Milan
Salgari E (1896) I pirati della Malesia. Vallardi, Milan
Sarfatti M (1926) Dux. Mondadori, Milan
Urso S (2003) Margherita Sarfatti. Dal mito del Dux al mito americano. Marsilio, Venice
Zanetti GF (2012) Astrology and race. Aspects of equality after critical race theory. Columbia J Race Law 2:267–278
Zanetti GF (2020) Filosofia de la vulnerabilidad. Percepción, Discriminación, Derecho. Dikynson, Madrid

Chapter 11
The Limits of Law and Arturo Carlo Jemolo's Islands

11.1 Italian Conscientious Objection

When the Italian Civil Unions law was enacted,[1] an uproar of outraged voices gave voice to some deep-seated conservative feelings, that had been simmering and bubbling during the public debate in the two Houses of the Parliament. Some conservative public figures, claimed that this new law was the definitive attack against "the family", and immediately announced that they were going to become conscientious objectors, i.e., they were not going to perform ceremonies of any kind for same sex couples.

Italians knew quite well what conscientious objection was about. The law that legalized women's reproductive rights had officially granted such an option for those doctors—mostly Catholic doctors—who did not want to perform abortions.[2] The most famous conscientious objection, nevertheless, was acknowledged, in the seventies, by a legal provision that finally allowed young men to claim that their religious or philosophical beliefs were incompatible with the military draft. It was only about men, because in those days women could not serve in the army.

The tale of this law is fascinating: it has to do with mutiny and desertions during World War I, with Jehovah's Witnesses and left-leaning priests in the sixties, with brave mayors and radical activists. It was finally approved in a duly watered-down version, the so-called "legge Marcora"[3]: young conscientious objectors could

---

This chapter was first discussed with the Fellows of the Townsend Center for Humanities in Berkeley, CA, on April 22, 2021. I would like to thank Timothy Hampton and all the Townsend Fellows for comments and suggestions. Special thanks I own to Albert Ascoli, Hans Lindahl, and Barbara Spackman, who kindly read the paper.

---

[1] L. May 20, 2016, n. 76, so-called "legge Cirinnà".

[2] L. May 22, 1978, n. 194, art. 9.

[3] L. December 15, 1972, n. 772.

G. Zanetti, *Equality and Vulnerability in the Context of Italian Political Philosophy*, Studies in the History of Law and Justice 26,
https://doi.org/10.1007/978-3-031-35553-0_11

choose an eight months longer civil service (than the usual year in uniform), if they were able to pass the scrutiny of an *ad hoc* committee, which was run by the Defense Ministry, i.e., by the Military. It was not a *right*, strictly speaking, but a *beneficio* that could be granted if specific conditions were met. One of such conditions, to be possibly verified by a stress interview, was the existence of such deeply seated beliefs—a Gandhian choice of non-violence, a sense of overriding religious obligation, feelings and beliefs which would have made the military service *impossible*, unacceptable, no matter what.

There is no longer in Italy a mandatory draft, but the fight of those activists did teach a lesson. When a law seems to go against a deep philosophical or religious belief, like the precious, valuable, unique difference between biological male and female (viciously denied by the Civil Unions Law), when those limits are crossed, there can be this last, extreme remedy.

The (most influential and learned) Catholic philosopher Francesco D'Agostino (2016) published an op-ed on *Avvenire*, the Newspaper of the CEI, the Italian Bishops Conference, attacking the law both from a legal and a moral point of view, but also incidentally stating that you do not fight an evil of this magnitude either with conscientious objection nor with a referendum. The conscientious objection project was then soon forgotten.[4]

11.2 "So Far As The Law Is Concerned"

Interestingly, one of the most traditional, formulaic, academic ways to frame the subject "limits of the law" has to do with gender in(equality), and it is somehow amusing that none of the scholars involved could have ever guessed how unwittingly prophetic their words were going to be. Norberto Bobbio, possibly the most outstanding legal philosopher in Italy, would start his reflections on the subject in such a classic way, i.e., quoting a famous line by De Lolme[5]:

> [p]arliament can do everything but make a woman a man and a man a woman.

What De Lolme had in mind was a factual "external" limit of the law, and he meant that Parliament can do anything at all, and the only limit is determined by what is impossible to accomplish anyway. De Lolme, however, should have perhaps chosen something impossible by definition, maybe one of the *impossibilia* mentioned by Umberto Eco in *Foucault's Pendulum*.[6] Another beloved (by some jurisprudence scholars) example of what is impossible to achieve by law is (together with

---

[4] D'Agostino (2016).

[5] De Lolme (2007).

[6] Eco (1988). See also Eco (1989) in the English translation by William Weaver (Secker & Warburg).

appointing Senator of Rome the emperor's favorite horse) the marriage between Nero and Sporus, as told for example by Suetonius.[7]

De Lolme, however, was keenly criticized by Sir Ivor Jennings, who seems to have had clearly in mind the distinction between *posse* and *licere*, between the "external limits of law" (there are outcomes that law cannot achieve because it is impossible—a legislative organ cannot do this, even if it may wish to do it), and the "internal limits of law" (those limits that have to do with the inner structure of a legal system—a legislative organ may not do this, even if it might be tempted to do it). Sir Ivor says[8]:

> [. . .] like many of the remarks de Lolme made, it is wrong. For if Parliament enacted that all men should be women then they would be women so far as the law was concerned.

Jennings was very much interested in unusual legal dilemmas, and he tried, for example, to determine if the English Parliament could legally forbid French citizens to smoke on the streets of Paris. It is worth remarking, however, that he is definitely not interested in the external limits of law. He is interested in a different point of view: sometimes law's words, like sacraments of the Catholic Church, *efficiunt quod figurant*, "they perform what they mean" *within their own normative sphere*.

So far as the law is concerned therefore means to give emphasis to the legal narrative and its autonomy—a narrative that does not necessarily look fully bound by any external reality.

The gender distinction conjured up by De Lolme hints at the *bios*, at the "natural" distinction between male and female, and it is meant to have roots in some notion of the "nature of things" themselves—it is therefore something that presents itself as hard, objective, and therefore unavailable to legal pressure. The narrative of objectivity and factual truth (that is sometimes assumed to dwell within scientific knowledge and method) expresses itself with a stern admonition: You can stretch and twist it as much as you want, but "a man is a man".

Critical Race Theory scholars have shown to a reluctant audience how race ascription (and the notion of race itself) can be quite arbitrary, even if it would routinely conjure up a scientific rhetoric of natural "distinctions".[9] The Vienna Bürgermeister, Karl Lüger, who most likely used anti-semitism as a populist banner (his was the offensive joke about Judapest, implying that the Jewish elite had control over the Hungarian capital), is said to have uttered those revealing words: "I decide who is a Jew". Can the Parliament decide "who is a man and who is a woman"?

The Archbishop of San Francisco, Salvatore Cordileone,[10] opposed same-sex marriage, comparing it with male breast feeding. His interview for the Orthodox Christian Program, Nectar, had as a capture-title "The Impossible Right"—not the

[7]Gaius Suetonius Tranquillus [121 AD] (2008) in the English translation by Catherine Edwards (Oxford University Press); see *Nero*, 28,1-2; 29, 1; 46, 1. See also Sextus Aurelius Victor, *Epitome de Caesaribus* 5, 7; Dio Cassius, *Epitome* LXII, 28.

[8]Jennings (1959), p. 170.

[9]Zanetti (2012), pp. 267–278.

[10]Cordileone (2013).

"excessive" right, not the "self-defeating" right, not the "most dangerous" right, but the "impossible" right. His line of argument does not rely on the authority of scriptures, on the *depositum fidei*, the magisterium, or on any (old and new) natural law theory: the right is said to be "impossible", and since it is impossible, you should not even think about it. In this narrative there are things which are beyond the grasp of law—things that are not ductile, flexible, plastic enough to be shaped the way law may wish to.

It is not just that it is an evil wish; it is more fundamentally an impossible wish, like the wish to live forever.

The compactness of legal narrative seems, however, to conjure up some kind of dreaded limitless power, but that ends up being just another name for its alleged autonomy, for the independence of its logic: *so far as the law was concerned.*

Mr. Cordileone would like to stress that the natural "world" (like the religious one) can stay beyond the grasp of any legal system, just as Lon Petrazycki's boa constrictor could strangle its owner, who legally speaking had full property rights on it, *ius utendi ac abutendi.*[11] From his point of view, spheres external to the almighty legal power seem immunized to such power: *illa se iaceat in aula!* This seems to imply a notion of *limits* of law as *borders*: there are lines in the sand that no Prince or Parliament can cross, and these lines are set by narratives external to legal systems (like science, or morality—in the old days it would have been natural law).

There is a most famous "special case", of course: sometimes it looks like it is the legal narrative itself that sets limits to the legal system. The classic, inevitable author to turn to is, once again, Georg Jellinek. The State "must", it "has to", limit itself (using its very power to perform such self-limiting action), in order to give itself a Constitution to which the state itself pre-exists.[12]

> If the State can, legally speaking, do anything, then it can dissolve the legal system, introduce anarchy, and make itself impossible. Nevertheless, if such a notion is to be rejected, then there will be a legal limit of the state with respect to the existence of an order. The State can of course choose the Constitution it will take, but it must eventually have a Constitution of some kind. Anarchy is within the sphere of factual possibility, not in the sphere of legal possibility.

From this point of view, it is in the sphere of *factual* possibility, that things can happen which cannot happen in the sphere of *legal* possibility, that is so vast and limitless you can keep it on the palm of one hand—its lack of limits is, in the case of Jellinek's self-limitation as well, another name for the relative autonomy it enjoys.

Carl Schmitt famously claimed that all the important public law notions come from theology. [13] Now, there should be no doubt that the notion of the limits of legal systems should qualify as *pregnant*, as important. Accordingly, one wonders if

[11] I would not have been aware of Petrazycki's vivid boa constrictor example but for the teaching of Enrico Pattaro. See Pattaro (1990), pp. 250–251. See Petrazycki (1955) in the translation by Hugh W. Babb., edited by Nicholas S. Timasheff (Harvard University Press).

[12] Jellinek (1960), p. 370.

[13] Schmitt (1922), p. 43.

Jellinek's vision, too, could qualify as political theology. It could be therefore interesting to remember, playing as it were Schmitt against Schmitt himself, that Georg Jellinek's father, Adolf, was a well-known Rabbi in Vienna—in the same years when Karl Lüger was Mayor—who taught at the Leopoldstädter Tempel, and who had thoroughly studied the medieval Spanish kabbalah author Samuel Ben Abulafia. One of first notions of a limitless power that sets limits to itself, in the Judeo-Christian tradition, could be that of *tzimtzum*, the God who "withdraws" Himself in the creation act. This notion is still to be found in authors like André Neher, [14] Hans Jonas, [15] Sergio Quinzio. [16] The family of Georg Jellinek was eventually going to be tragically attacked by a power that was not setting any limit on itself—during the *shoah* his children, Walter and Dora, were deported to Theresienstadt, while Otto died because of the beatings inflicted by the Gestapo.

The fate of Jellinek's family, even more than his theoretical position, seems to require a subtler scrutiny of the problem.

11.3 Borders and Limits of the Law

Such a subtler scrutiny could be facilitated by a philosophy of law that boldly *contrasts* the notion of limits with (rather than assimilates it to) that more intuitive idea of the borders of law. Rather than thinking of limits (of law) in terms of borders, it could be "the notion of a limit that one should be looking at when conceptualizing spatial closure and spatial inclusion and exclusion, not borders"—a notion for example recently submitted by Hans Lindahl[17] (and that was here first used while discussing Dante[18]).

Lindahl starts out from the dilemmas posed by globalization processes, that take the form of an inclusion/exclusion system, despite their envisioning a utopian "interior without exterior," an inside without an outside. A global legal order could indeed constitute an inside without an outside, if that distinction could be predicated solely on borders, or frontiers.

The law, at any rate, necessarily sets up a distinction between its *own* space and a foreign state's space. While the distinction between domestic and foreign may be contingent in relation to legal orders, and of doubtful existence when it comes to globalized orders, the distinction between one's "own" space and a "strange" space (a space of the "stranger") is an ineluctable necessity. These orders, in other words, cannot refrain from putting an inclusion/exclusion dynamic into effect, even when

[14] Neher (1970).

[15] Jonas (1987).

[16] Quinzio (1993).

[17] Lindahl (2018), p. 28.

[18] See in this volume, *Dante Alighieri, Hans Kelsen, and the* principium unitatis.

this dynamic does not take on the exterior form of a geographical space marked by borders that divide and order it.

We already tried to shed some light on the complexity of the problem by following Lindahl in discussing a distinction between "world" and "globe". The spatiality of the globe is thought of as a surface—the so-called face of the earth—represented in geographical maps and terrestrial globes (*mappa mundi*). In virtue of that spherical surface of the globe, space essentially becomes extension; ergo, global legal orders are spatial in the sense that they literally have a *boundless* extension.

Of course, *world* and *globe* can be taken as synonyms, and then the world simply becomes a *res extensa*. But we already found out that such a *world* is not a thing. It would be a category mistake to equate the world with the globe, because the former, but not the latter, is not "a very large thing nor even the totality of all things" but is instead "a nexus of meaningful relations *co*given and *pre*given with all the things, events and acts that populate it[19]."

The world exists relative to a subject. Boundaries may belong to the globe, but they are not pertinent to a world: a world has limits, and it is when different worlds intersect that, predictably, the limit of a legal space becomes apparent, and does so even vividly.

A city that occupies a portion of geographical territory and is delimited on a map is an *urbs*: it has boundaries and is an object of investigation for geography and (appropriately enough) urban studies. A city located in an Arendtian[20] territory, in Lindahl's spatiality of the world, is a *civitas*: it interprets itself through the lens of legal institutions and is an object of investigation for normative philosophy. The notion of *civitas*—the complex of citizens and their normative self-interpretation—does not entail any neat boundaries (citizens residing abroad are fully citizens, whether in a political, legal, cultural, or existential sense) but it does always entail an inclusion/exclusion dynamic, and one that can be deeply painful.[21]

So, there can exist legal orders that are borderless but not limitless (global orders); there can be legal systems that are borderless, but not without at the same time constructing an inside and an outside, that is, not without setting up a concrete inclusion/exclusion dynamic. Institutions do not imply any Universal Equality conceived as a stable, graspable entity (although they can claim just that).

The point is not just theoretical. Lindahl mentions the violent resistance the Karnataka State Farmers' Association (KKRS) in India has mounted against the farming of genetically modified crops under the aegis of the World Trade Organization (WTO): in this conflict, the WTO embodies a global order, where it sees itself

[19] Lindahl (2018), p. 35.

[20] See in this volume, *Dante Alighieri, Hans Kelsen, and the* principium unitatis.

[21] When the Romans took the city of Capua, they decided it should exist as an *urbs* (Livy 26.16) but they destroyed the *civitas*, understood as the political structure of the laws and the magistracies. A worse and more famous fate befell Carthage, which was allowed to retain its laws—the *civitas* was spared—but the *urbs* was forcibly moved inland, and the great city of Carthage was destroyed, as we learn from Appian of Alexandria, *Roman History*, bk. VIII (The Punic Wars), 89, in the speech delivered by Consul Censorinus. Cp. Brett (2018), pp. 23–42.

as occupying an inside—the global market it configures as its own space—all the while excluding (as lying *outside* this space) other kinds of positions that are deemed irrelevant. These marginalized positions, however, take the form of behaviors that challenge the practice of configuring space in a way that is alien, or *extraneous*, to their *own* configuration of space (the traditional one of Indian villages), being foreign to the local self-understanding of what constitutes a community as a common place.[22]

> To experience the limits of a legal order is not merely to be aware of the fact that there are "other" ways of ordering behavior, as when I know *in abstracto* that there are a host of legal orders "out there," but rather to be confronted, *here*, with another way of ordering space that challenges the commonality of what I had taken to be "our" space.[23]

This understanding of legal pluralism takes on a radical edge when we consider that the mere availability of another narrative within that *here* inevitably modifies the web of meanings that constitutes a normative given world: the WTO is no longer the same thing once a formal pronouncement is made, recognizing that it can *also* be understood as an entity whose activity can be rightly challenged through the use of violence, even if we do not agree with that assessment. Family too, was no longer the same, once it had been challenged by minority groups who would point out their exclusion, re-shaping the legal narrative "from within".

And therefore, it is certainly true that, as Lindahl pithily observes, "the experience of the limit of a legal order is the experience of legal pluralisation.[24]" But this is not a problem that only applies to global orders, namely, to those orders that, ideally, exist independently of any geographical boundary. The statement equally applies to normative systems *in general*: they *all* can harbor alternative narratives that live *within* them.

11.4 Incompatible Narratives

This brings us back where we first started. Conscientious objection per se is no limit of law: *it is law* (if performed *secundum legem*, according to the law; if it is *contra legem*, i.e., performed in violation of the law, it is no limit of the law either, it is a crime). The above-mentioned Italian law, however, did graciously grant the possibility of avoiding the draft only to those young men who were able to convince the members of a military committee that they would deem the military service as an unviable, unacceptable option, a course of action which was to be refused no matter what.

This means that the law was granting legal meaning (an *Anerkennung*, a recognition, of some kind) to a narrative that was utterly incompatible with its own. From

[22] Lindahl (2018), p. 24.
[23] Lindahl (2018), p. 38.
[24] Lindahl (2018), p. 39.

the point of view of the objectors, holding deadly weapons in their arms was *unacceptable, period*—what the law could state on the subject was not a decisive factor in their decision-making process, although they were willing to take advantage of it. From their point of view, actually, the law "had to" grant this opportunity. From the point of view of the legal narrative, on the other hand, those young men could be objectors only because of the *octroyée* legal permission, which nevertheless implied the recognition of a narrative utterly incompatible with its own. The test was passed only when the candidate was found to be sincere, i.e., when his motives were based on a notion of legal system incompatible with the notion of legal system on which the law itself was based. This is where *worlds* collide, where incompatible narratives live one within the other. In these interstitial spaces between narratives dwells a notion of limits of law that is perhaps not graspable by any geographic border metaphor.

There is no denying that these arguments, once drawn into the permissive rule that allows the objection, are themselves an expression of the law's unlimited power; it is equally undeniable, however, that the same arguments, recognized by law, bear the import of a radical challenge, and rest on a different narrative that finds itself incompatibly at odds with the narrative of the law.

In this case, the law's limit does not lie in a boundary that keeps us from what is "beyond the pale," such as what is in violation of natural law—a normative boundary marked by the Pillars of Hercules—but rather lies in the interstitial space where incompatible narratives overlap.

Worlds can overlap whose narratives are incompatible as to their logic, but whose interaction enables *both* narratives to survive. The law is impure because, in the case at hand, it dresses in legal garb the very thing that denies it the power to dress that thing in legal garb. Beccaria's gentlemen, ready to duel in order to defend their honor faced a similar predicament.[25]

11.5 Rocks Among the Waves

Once the intuitive notion of the limits of law as borders is removed, there is an opening for those interstitial spaces created by the overlapping of powerful, and contested, narratives.

It is therefore a double irony that the most famous legal metaphor on the limits of law is both geographical and "catholic"—because catholic was its author, Arturo Carlo Jemolo, who penned one of the most wildly famous quotes in Italian jurisprudence.

[25] See in this volume, *Cesare Beccaria and the Narrative of Neutral Equality*, Sect. 7.3.

Under some circumstances, according to Jemolo, when some subjects are at stake, there emerge those famous *islands* "which the sea of the law can lap against, but can only lap against." The "sea of the law" can, *should*, never submerge them.[26]

> The family is the rock among waves, and the granite which forms the bedrock belongs to the world of the affects, to the primary instincts, to morality, to religion, not to the world of the law.

What bears mentioning here is the heterogeneity of the spheres that, in this connection, make up the family's granitic "bedrock": intuitively, we might say, it is not necessarily the case that the "primary instincts" are, as it were, entirely syntonic with "morality" and "religion"—in fact I suspect that they could perhaps occasionally unsettle an orderly conjugal ménage. Jemolo is somehow conjuring up the alternative narratives that he feels are competing with the legal one when the notion of family is at stake.

The "family", therefore, may well be an island—not in the *globe* though, nor in any bordered normative horizon, but in the *world*, in that nexus of meanings that can include alternative narratives, different possibilities. Efficacy phenomena can therefore exist on the background of a pluralism of narratives; such narratives do not need to be compatible one with another. This is why vulnerable groups (objectors, gay men and women fighting for a right to marry) can engage in equality practices, and try to will into existence a different, more inclusive, normative narrative.

References

Brett B (2018) Is there any place for environmental thinking in early modern European political thought? In: Forrester K, Smith S (eds) Nature, action and the future: political thought and the environment. Cambridge University Press, Cambridge, pp 23–42

Cordileone S (2013) A Conversation on Same Sex "Marriage" with Archbishop Salvatore Cordileone, Roman Catholic Archdiocese of San Francisco. Patristic Nectar Publications (PNP), youTube. https://www.youtube.com/watch?v=XcS42gWhZ5w

D'Agostino F (2016) Unioni civili, ora e sempre resilienza. Avvenire. 12 May

De Lolme J-L (2007) In: Lieberman D (ed) The constitution of England; or, an account of the English Government. Indianapolis, Liberty Fund

Eco U (1988) Il pendolo di Foucault. Bompiani, Milano. English edition: Eco U (1989) Foucault's Pendulum (trans: Weaver W). Secker & Warburg, London

Gaius Suetonius Tranquillus (2008) In: Edwards C (ed) Lives of the caesars. Oxford University Press, Oxford

Jellinek G (1960) Allgemeine Staatslehere. Wissenschaftliche Buchgesellschaft, Darmstad

Jemolo A-C (1957) La famiglia e il diritto. In: Scavo Lombardo L (ed) Pagine sparse di diritto e storiografia. Giuffrè, Milan

Jennings I (1959) The law and the constitution. University of London Press, London

Jonas A (1987) Der Gottesbegriff nach Auschwitz. Suhrkamp, Frankfurt

Lindahl H (2018) Authority and the globalisation of inclusion and exclusion. Cambridge University Press, Cambridge

[26] Jemolo (1957), p. 241.

Neher A (1970) L'exil de la parole. Du silence biblique au silence d'Auschwitz. Seuil, Paris
Pattaro E (1990) Introduzione al corso di filosofia del diritto. CLUEB, Bologna
Petrazycki L (1955) Law and morality. In: Timasheff NS (ed) (trans: Babb H-W). Harvard University Press, Cambridge
Quinzio S (1993) La sconfitta di Dio. Adelphi, Milan
Schmitt C (1922) Politische Theologie, Vier Kapitel zur Lehre der Souveranität. Duncker & Humblot, München-Leipzig
Zanetti GF (2012) Astrology and race. Aspects of equality after critical race theory. Columb J Race Law 2:267–278

Chapter 12
The Italian "Braibanti Affaire": A Tale of Two Vulnerabilities

12.1 A Landmark Case

Vulnerability is currently a notion in good stand with the scholarly community, thanks to the work of outstanding scholars like Martha Fineman. [1] The idea of this Chapter is to focus on vulnerabilit*ies*, in the plural and more precisely on *situated* vulnerabilities—i.e., forms of vulnerabilities that are not to be explained by some notion of human nature, by an anthropology, or any metaphysics, but exclusively in the background of the contingent narratives that radiate from some given forms of discrimination. The assumption, therefore, is that each vulnerability can be and is essentially unique, and different from any other.

While it can make a lot of good sense to forbid discrimination based on sex, gender, "race", sexual orientation, and so on, it remains true that vulnerabilities figures are not like primary colors, or chemical elements—they are, each of them can be, the product of contingent arrays of efficacy circumstances.

As a somehow unwelcome consequence, it is not that, once you have the full list of candidates to vulnerability status and discrimination, you can take the required steps to (try to) protect them. Because there is no such list. As a matter of fact, sometimes vulnerability phenomena are so intense that become invisible, part of the very normative horizon we take for granted—Giambattista Vico's plebeians, his *famuli*, valiantly fought for equality, universal equality of course, that they finally achieved when Roman Citizenship was granted to all those who would dwell within

My heartfelt thanks are due to Barbara Spackman, who carefully read this paper and encouraged me with precious corrections.

[1] Albertson Fineman (2004, 2008).

G. Zanetti, *Equality and Vulnerability in the Context of Italian Political Philosophy*, Studies in the History of Law and Justice 26,
https://doi.org/10.1007/978-3-031-35553-0_12

the borders of the Roman Empire—but needless to say, Vico was not really thinking of women.[2]

I would like to describe here a concrete, real life case of vulnerability—embracing, as it were, a bottom-up approach. It is a landmark case, a terrible tale of Italian legal and cultural cruelty, and has to do with a most famous legal norm, that Penal Code article that would harshly punish *plagiarism.*

This landmark case shaped Italian normative horizon in a unique way—nothing was ever going to be the same after that. It had to do not just with law, but with love too; it forced a reluctant audience to discuss contemporary art, and literature; it conjured up the Italian fascist past, and the current political dilemmas; it did set one against the other two kinds of vulnerabilities. The case, as I said, was about the crime of plagio.

The word "plagiarism", in English, means: "the process or practice of using another person's ideas or work and pretending that it is your own". In Italian "plagio" means the same thing. Even in the field of Jurisprudence or Philosophy of Law, there have been in Italy some cruel scandals: a few years ago, one of the key Italian figures had to resign from a lofty academic position, because one of his published papers was but a translation of a rather famous article by Odo Marquard.

Until a few years ago, however, in Italy, the word *plagio* had another penal law related meaning. *Plagio* was a specific crime: a mental influence on an innocent, weaker mind, who would find himself or herself in state of subjection, almost brainwashed.

Plagio, in the Italian Law, was the subject-matter of art. 603 of the Penal Code:

> Chiunque sottopone una persona al proprio potere, in modo da ridurla in totale stato di soggezione, è punito con la reclusione da cinque a quindici anni.

The legal provision was a creation of the Codice Rocco, the Penal Code enacted during the Fascist regime: "Whoever subjects another person to his own power, in order to put him in a total state of subjection, is punished with a reclusion from five to fifteen years".

The Italian Supreme Court found this Penal Code provision at odds with our Constitution (96, June 8 1981). Before this article was canceled, however, it was used to condemn and to punish, after World War II, only *once*. The name of the felon was Aldo Braibanti.[3]

---

[2]See in this volume, *Introduction,* Sect. 1.1 and *Paradoxes of Equality: Giambattista Vico.*

[3]Raffo and Braibanti (2003) and Pacini (2016). Aldo Braibanti in Nomadica: http://www.nomadica.eu/aldo-braibanti.

12.2 A Tale of Two Vulnerabilities

Braibanti had been active in the Resistance Movement against the Germans and the fascists; his first contributions against the fascist regime, indeed, date to his high school days. Braibanti joined the Resistenza when he was studying philosophy at the University of Florence.

He first gave his allegiance to the *Giustizia and Libertà* (Justice and Freedom) movement, and later he switched to Communist Party. The switch had little to do with any ideological reason: son of a doctor, Braibanti felt the need to connect with other social classes, and perceived the key role that the labor problem was going to play in Italy. It must be stressed that Braibanti's loyalty to the Anti-Fascist movement was no joke: he was arrested twice, in 1943 (they released him on July 25, at the downfall of Fascism itself, when General Badoglio ordered that Professors and Students could go free), and in 1944 by the Fascists of notorious Banda Carità, so reckless and cruel to be frown upon even by the philosopher Giovanni Gentile (the official thinker of Fascism, who joined the Repubblica di Salò just like Carità did, and who was later killed because of the role he played during the Fascist years). Many papers by Braibanti were seized by German SS soldiers and were lost forever.[4]

It is interesting to remark that, after having served in the Italian Communist Party in Tuscany, he elected to withdraw from active political life—he did so, by the way, with a short poem published by the *Il Ponte* journal. "It is no adieu"—he wrote—"it is a leave".

Braibanti was an out-of-the-mainstream intellectual, with a variety of interests: art, politics, poetry. His main artistic interests were probably the *collage* and the *objet d'art trouvé.*[5]

He was a self-made scientist, too, and his interest for some species of ants, and for social insects in general, was never a superficial hobby. This interest was somehow linked to an early, keen environmental sensibility: Among his teen-ager poetic productions there are "hymns to nature".

He was also a writer, author of theatre pieces. For six years he was part of an extraordinary community, an art laboratory within a Farnese *torrione* (old tower) in Castell'Arquato. The works, often ceramics, created by the members of such community, have been in several exhibitions, both in Italy and in US.

Braibanti moved to Rome in 1962: his artistic and literary activity thrived in contact with artists like Sylvano Bussotti and Marco Bellocchio. He was then charged with *plagio*, and condemned, in 1968—sometimes years are important.

Braibanti, by the way, did not start any cult, he would not use any technique usually mastered by self-appointed gurus. He was an atheist, and of course his ideas were quite leftist – but he denounced the Stalinist trends he would perceive within

[4]The fact that Braibanti had been a *partigiano* was never forgotten. In this regard see: Letteratura, è morto l'artista e partigiano Aldo Braibanti, "La Repubblica", 8 April 2014. https://bologna.repubblica.it/cronaca/2014/04/08/news/letteratura_morto_aldo_braibanti-83062547/.

[5]Braibanti (1979).

the Italian Communist Party. He was, in Pier Paolo Pasolini's words, "meek"[6]; the actor Carmelo Bene, who had personally known him, stated that he was "the best" Italian intellectual of his age.[7] And he was gay.[8]

The facts are quite simple. Braibanti went to Rome with a young man, 23 years old, Giovanni Sanfratello, whose family was extremely conservative (they had been close to the Fascist regime), and very "pious", i.e., Catholic. Giovanni went to Rome with Braibanti, most likely, to escape from such a closed, suffocating domestic environment. Giovanni's father, Ippolito Sanfratello, took legal action charging Braibanti with *plagio*: according to Ippolito, Braibanti had managed to insinuate himself in the mind of his naïf son, conquering his trust, poisoning his heart with twisted ideas and feelings, with an attitude that worked like a powerful mind control device.

Four people violently abducted Giovanni from the cheap Hotel where he was living with Braibanti. He was taken, against his will, first to a private clinic in Modena and then to the Verona mental hospital. The Italian writer Alberto Moravia informed his readers that Giovanni Sanfratello was then subjected to several electroshocks and several insulin shocks. He was, by force, prevented from contacting a lawyer, or his friends. He was dismissed after 15 months.

The papers signed by the doctors who "treated" Sanfratello are worth a Netflix horror series. Two conditions prescribed *by doctors* to allow Giovanni to leave the mental hospital were (a) forced domicile at his parents', and (b) the prohibition to read any book published *less than hundred years ago*. During the trial, Giovanni Sanfratello managed to state that never had Braibanti tried to force him to do anything—Braibanti had not subjugated him.

Italian trials take a notoriously long time. After four years of legal procedures, Braibanti was eventually condemned to serve time, 9 years.[9] An Appellate Court later managed a reduction of the sentence. He did serve two years in jail, however, and 2 years were pardoned because of his deeds during the *Resistenza* movement against the fascist regime and the Germans.

Umberto Eco produced a long, detailed, painstaking analysis of the trial.[10] The language used by Braibanti's accusers was keenly scrutinized: in a nutshell, it became apparent that it had been a political trial, with Braibanti as a scapegoat. A witch trial—these are not words by Eco—had managed to condemn an Italian citizen not for anything he had actually done, but for who and what he was—a bohemian, a gay man, an artist, an intellectual, a communist and the things for which he stood.

---

[6] Pasolini (1969).

[7] See Bene and Dotto (1998).

[8] Pini (2011).

[9] Finzi Ghisi (1968) and Ferluga (2003). See the trial proceedings: Braibanti (1969) *La sentenza Braibanti* (De Donato).

[10] Moravia et al. (1969). I would like to thank Diego Cuoghi for having sent me this text during the first Covid-19 lockdown; Eco (2012).

Cesare Musatti, one of the founders of the Italian Freudian psychoanalysis, pointed out that any Freudian orthodox psychoanalyst could have been charged with *plagio* by any patient quitting the therapy during the transference, because of that characteristic dependence patients almost always develop for their "shrink". Ginevra Bompiani, Alberto Moravia, and many others took a clear position as well.[11]

Conservative journalists basked in the pleasure of attacking, with a dismissive attitude, "the usual intellectuals", always ready to take sides in favor of those who are eager to defile Italian shared morality, and the traditional values. A key role was played by out-of-the mainstream politicians like Marco Pannella, leader of the small but inspired *Partito Radicale*.

In the end it did not work. Braibanti, a free man again, kept his usual low profile, writing and working. His contribution is now officially acknowledged. He lived his last years in poverty, although he was granted the financial help provided by the so called Bacchelli law, a special provision that grants a small salary to extremely poor Italians with special merits in the field of art or literature.[12] Evicted from his Rome home, he moved back to the village where he had grown up.

It was probably because of the blatant, cruel injustice perpetrated in the Braibanti affaire that the Italian *Corte Costituzionale* eventually decided that the Penal Code article that punished *plagio* was to be deemed as at odds with Italian Constitution. From this point of view, Braibanti had the last word: he was the first, and the last one, to be charged of *plagio*.[13]

This is a tale of two vulnerabilities. The judicial establishment happily accepted the ready-made narrative about Giovanni Sanfratello's vulnerability. The fellow was a good guy, born and raised in a traditional family, but he was naive, exposed as it were to the malicious influence of a sinister and ambiguous individual. Sanfratello was vulnerable for two reasons. First, he was vulnerable as an individual. His character was not strong, or at least he had not been strong enough to shield himself against the creepy slow action poison that radiated from Braibanti. As a matter of fact, the fatal encounter had happened to him—exposure to Braibanti was a ill-starred event that could have spoiled most lives, and yet it had been Giovanni's fate to meet his doom disguised as an artist and intellectual. Number two, Giovanni Sanfratello was vulnerable because he was an ordinary Joe, a member of that majority of Italians who could live, if left alone, a happy and decent life: he was born in an appropriately conservative and Christian family, and all what he needed in order to find his way was to be protected by external, dangerous influences.

[11] Moravia et al. (1969).

[12] L 8 August 1985, n. 440; the writer Bacchelli could not take any advantage from such an opportunity, because he died only two months after the law was passed.

[13] The full text of the landmark decision of the Corte Costituzionale (decision 1981/96, 8 June) is available at: https://www.cortecostituzionale.it/actionSchedaPronuncia.do?param_ecli=ECLI:IT:COST:1981:96.

Most parents would have been concerned that their own son (or daughter) could by chance run into one of these mesmeric, sinister characters. The silent, decent majority is often helpless in front of the cunning and the malice of those few masters of sin and doubt, just like most mortals have no defense against the spell of some cruel witch.

There is then a second vulnerability at stake here—Braibanti's vulnerability. It is a different kind of vulnerability. Braibanti belonged to a minority, *rectius*, to several minorities. He was not just a pure, mere, "naked" individual, trialed and judged because of external actions. He was an encumbered, *situated* individual, whose identity was clearly framed in the spiral of overlapping minority groups to which he belonged.

First, he was a bohemian—I use this term for lack of a better word. He had not followed the shared guidelines of decent social conduct in the Italy of the sixties: he had not married, he had not found a "proper" job, and so on.

Second, he was an atheist—in those years, it was not so much religion as fact of faith that was requested to be socially acceptable, but religion as a fact of culture: it was an identity, linked to a formal respect for some social hierarchies.

Third, he was an intellectual—during his years of University in Florence he had particularly loved Giordano Bruno and Baruch Spinoza. These two philosophers are quite different from each other, but they were both dissenters, they both had big problems with the religious establishment, they both were found outrageous by their fellow co-citizens.

Fourth, he was gay.[14] Sanfratello was of age, and that prevented other charges against Braibanti: but his homosexuality was always present in the mind of Sanfratello's father, Ippolito, of the accusers, and of the public audience who would read about the *affaire* in the newspapers. Being gay was a direct violation of the virility norm, something perceived as a shameful condition of degradation, if not a full-fledged abomination. Interestingly, in the accuser's harangue, Braibanti's homosexuality is conjured up to state its irrelevance for the case at hand—a clever rhetorical move, since consensual homosexual behavior was not illegal in Italy: *plagio* had nothing to do with sexual orientation, and yet everybody was deftly reminded that the accused one was a gay man.

Fifth, he was an artist. His art was *contemporary* art, of course. It was meant to be avant-garde and somehow revolutionary. It was an activity and a vocation specifically irking for the mainstream Italian bourgeoisie, who would often feel a moral revulsion in front of the strangeness, and the deliberate inherent provocation, of an outrageous artistic production whose meaning was ungraspable and obscure. During the trial, Braibanti's artistic skills and achievements were questioned and mocked.

Sixth, he was a leftist, and a former card-carrying communist. In the years of the cold war, it was not without a political meaning that a demonic corrupter of the youth

[14] I write these words holding my breath—human lives can be complex, fluid, sometimes difficult to grasp. Interviewed by Felix Cossolo, Braibanti stated that neither Sanfratello nor he had ever "ruled out women". See Cossolo (1979).

was a commie. This kind of vulnerability was double-edged, because the official position of the Communist Party was that homosexuality was a bourgeoisie perversion, a social disease that infected the Western, capitalist societies. Braibanti was therefore exposed to a further discrimination within the very circle of his political allegiance and former affiliation.

Seventh, Braibanti belonged to all these minority groups *at the same time*, therefore embodying the perfect victim for a resentful conservative society, that desperately needed to shed his legal and institutional blood in order to assert a social hierarchy that was perceived as unstable and shaky. He embodied special case of intersectional vulnerability.

Braibanti was a white man, but there was a racist hint in the papers of his trial. One of the witnesses for the prosecution stated that Braibanti had told him about a sexual relationship he (Braibanti) had had with a black man, and how he had enjoyed it. There is no comment on this revelation, but the subtext is almost palpable—the man was at the deepest circle of human degradation, and the very notion that innocent young men could be exposed to such tales was probably enough a reason to condemn the monster no matter what.

From the point of view of this second, situated vulnerability, Giovanni Sanfratello was vulnerable for the very same reasons Braibanti was: he was an artist (or someone interested in becoming one), a young intellectual, somebody who had chosen to share with Braibanti a bohemian lifestyle (at least for a while), a young man who was critically examining the religious tradition in which he had grown, and who was probably exploring his sexual potential, while processing the leftist ideas to which he had been exposed.

12.3 Vulnerability and Equality Practices

Both Aldo Braibanti and Giovanni Sanfratello paid the price for their minority identities, although the power of two different institutions was unleashed against them. Giovanni Sanfratello was attacked by the medical "white" power—here white has no "racial" meaning, but it hints at the symbol of that social power, the doctor's garb, the medical gown. In those years white was the color of hospitals of any kind—the open explanation was that it was easier to detect any possible dirt or dust, obviously dangerous for the patients. No doctor ever paid any price neither for the abduction and the imprisonment of a young adult, a man of (young) age capable of understanding and willing, nor for the tortures to which he was submitted. Aldo Braibanti, on the other hand, had to face another repressive institution, and suffered a different imprisonment, in a jail.[15]

It is possible to disentangle two different meanings that can be given to the word/concept vulnerability *as far as the Braibanti case is concerned*. Giovanni was

[15] Braibanti (1969).

perceived by his father and by the Italian institutions as vulnerable *as an individual*: he had just been maliciously pushed, or pulled, out of the mainstream. A Mental Hospital, therefore, had to put it back where he belonged. Giovanni needed to be fixed. It was mandatory to keep him in a sanitized cultural environment, in order to prevent any influence from the outside world, perceived as potentially dangerous. This vulnerability is linked to a given (if crass) anthropology: it is that human vulnerability all human beings share, the inherent fragility of a mortal and limited existence. We all can have a moment of weakness (although some of us can be more susceptible to such moments), and we must pray not to run into a "Braibanti character" when this happens. We all could be Giovanni Sanfratello, especially our kids could.

Braibanti's vulnerability can be conceptualized in a different way. Such a vulnerability is not linked to any anthropology: it is different from that human vulnerability all human beings share. Braibanti did not need to be *fixed*. He had to be punished, basically because of who and what he was—an individual member of specific groups. This vulnerability has therefore to do with *vulnerability figures*, not with an unencumbered human being, and not even with a sanitized abstract notion of "citizen" in a liberal democracy. It is a situated vulnerability—linked to groups and identities, and to contingent inclusion/exclusion dynamics.

There is so much at stake here. The first kind of vulnerability is compatible with a notion of social health. When everybody is acting according to given shared values, the social and legal system is a healthy one, because no limb or organ is liable to be attacked by any cultural virus. The second kind of vulnerability is not compatible with such a notion of social health. There is no health, only diseases (discrimination phenomena) and therapies (equality practices whose goal is to fight that given discrimination), but there is no formula, no recipe of universal equality, because such an equality is linked to perceived vulnerable figures, the outcome of a non-neutral, contingent narrative that nevertheless presents itself as objective.

This means that the former option is compatible with legal moralism, i.e., with the notion that the legal system can and should try to make men (and women) moral; with legal paternalism, i.e., with the notion that the legal system knows what is the citizens' best interest better than the citizens themselves. It is quite an ambitious, but reassuring, program: we can take care of social health, and happiness, just by healing the poisoned members of our community and removing the poisoners from it.[16]

The second option is compatible with a notion of individual autonomy, and is not able to offer any such reassuring picture. All what we are left with is a keen feeling of the relevance of our listening skills, so that we can detect those situated vulnerabilities that are dwelling within our normative horizon. Since no definitive universal equality is available from this point of view, what is valuable is no longer the (comparatively) short distance that separates us from an ideal situation of social health, based on a shared anthropology, but only the contingent respect we may have

[16]The poisoner, i.e. the "monster". Coppola (1996).

for those subaltern counterpublics[17] that perceive (and help us to perceive) some given situated vulnerability phenomena.

The Braibanti affaire was therefore a landmark normative case. Now, from a merely legal point of view, the personal life of Aldo Braibanti was crushed by the vicious injustice to which he had been subjected. While this statement is, per se, accurate, it actually hides more than it reveals. The workings of normative systems are sometimes strange and convoluted. Both a judicial landmark opinion and the enactment of a statute are legal phenomena. They can be, and are, very different from the point of view of the unlucky one who finds himself caught in the snares of a repressive institution. As far as the history of Italian jurisprudence is concerned, however, the Braibanti *affaire* backfired in quite an interesting way. First, the unfairness of the trial, and the commitment of leading figures in the Italian *intelligentsia*, was certainly a motivating factor for that landmark sentence of the Italian *Corte Costituzionale* that repealed the law.

Number two, the very fact that, under the Prodi administration, Braibanti was granted financial assistance under the *Legge Bacchelli* umbrella, meant a public acknowledgment of his contribution, and an unofficial apology for the unfair trial. The prosecutors had tried to ridicule Braibanti, questioning his art, his ideology, his cultural achievements. The decision taken by the Prodi administration was a normative overriding of those insulting words.

The Braibanti *affaire* had taught a lesson: there are citizens who, because of the encompassing groups to which they belong, are more easily subject of discrimination; they are *specifically* vulnerable to *different* kinds of attack. Such vulnerabilities figures are to be understood in the background of contingent efficacy circumstances, and of the *world* willed into existence together with the legitimizing narratives that those phenomena radiate; they are, however, conceptualized like this because an alternative narrative is simmering, herald of more inclusive identities and institutions, that will crystallize new shared beliefs.

Italian equal protection law had taken some timid, fearful baby steps. There was and there is still a long way to go, but, well, big things have small beginnings.

References

Albertson Fineman M (2004) The autonomy myth: a theory of dependency. The New Press, New York

Albertson Fineman M (2008) The vulnerable subject: anchoring equality in the human condition. Yale J Law Feminism 20(1):1–23

Bene C, Dotto G (1998) Vita di Carmelo Bene. Bompiani, Milan

Braibanti A (1969) Le prigioni di Stato. Feltrinelli, Milan

Braibanti A (1979) Objets trouvés. Stamperia della Bezuga, Florence

[17] See in this volume, *Equality and Vulnerability in* The Duties of Man*: Giuseppe Mazzini*, Sect. 8.3.

Coppola F (1996) L'ultimo 'mostro' prima di Valpreda. La Repubblica, 8 November. https://ricerca.repubblica.it/repubblica/archivio/repubblica/1996/11/08/ultimo-mostro-prima-di-valpreda.html

Cossolo F (1979) Il caso Aldo Braibanti. Lambda. January-February https://www.culturagay.it/saggio/144

Eco U (2012) Il costume di casa. Evidenze e misteri dell'ideologia italiana negli anni sessanta. Bompiani, Milan

Ferluga G (2003) Il processo Braibanti. Zamorani, Turin

Finzi Ghisi V (1968) Il caso Braibanti ovvero un processo di famiglia. Feltrinelli, Milan

Moravia A et al (1969) Sotto il nome di plagio. Bompiani, Milan

Pacini P (2016) Fuori tempo. Intervista ad Aldo Braibanti. Carmignani Editrice, Cascina (Pisa)

Pasolini P-P (1969) Il Tempo: 33 (13 August)

Pini A (2011) Quando eravamo froci. Gli omosessuali nell'Italia di una volta. Il Saggiatore, Milan

Raffo S, Braibanti A (2003). Emergenze. Conversazioni con Aldo Braibanti. Vicolo del Pavone, Piacenza

Chapter 13
We, the People: Of Poets and Priests. Pasolini's Very Hard Poem

13.1 Pasolini's Poem

Every legal and political "we" can turn into quite a challenge, and it can often overlap with nationalist, organic notions of the political body. The Italian Vincenzo Cuoco was compared to Edmund Burke by Benedetto Croce: according to Cuoco the reason for the failed Naples revolution was that it had been carried out following the blueprint of the French Revolution, in reckless disregard of the peculiar Italian spirit, of the historical concrete reality of the country, of the spiritual differences.[1]

Needless to say, Italian identity is difficult to elaborate because there are so many differences between its regions: it is not much bigger than California, and yet it comprises both the Alps and Sicily. Most of its cities have been, for some centuries, capitals of important political units, endowed with their own mores, laws, customs, literature, cuisine, and so on. The poet (writer, movie director and intellectual) Pier Paolo Pasolini offered one of the most severe notions of the Italian character.

L'intelligenza non avrà mai peso, mai
nel giudizio di questa pubblica opinione.
Neppure sul sangue dei lager, tu otterrai

da uno dei milioni d'anime della nostra nazione,
un giudizio netto, interamente indignato:
irreale è ogni idea, irreale ogni passione,

di questo popolo ormai dissociato [...].

[1] Cuoco [1802] (2014) in the English translation by David Gibbons, edited and with an introduction by Bruce Haddock and Filippo Sabetti (Toronto University Press). See Viglione (2016), pp. 197–226.

G. Zanetti, *Equality and Vulnerability in the Context of Italian Political Philosophy*, Studies in the History of Law and Justice 26,
https://doi.org/10.1007/978-3-031-35553-0_13

The title of the poem is *Italians*[2] and it is pretty bad.

Intelligence will never matter, ever,
In the judgment of this public opinion.
Not even in the blood of concentration camps you will find,

from one among the million souls of our nation,
A clearly cut judgment, entirely outraged:
All ideas are unreal, unreal any passion,

Of this now alienated people [...].

Pasolini deliberately revives a tradition of civil critique: outrage at the lack of outrage, authentic revolt against lack of authenticity and deep feelings in a country that had already been well described by, among others, Gerolamo Cardano's *Prosseneta*. And yet, it looks like it is still possible to speak of Italians, if only to charge them with moral indolence and cynicism; the lack of ideals and passions could perhaps be the last shared value of a dwindling identity, a people *dissociato*, i.e., alienated from itself, without any inherent unity principle. The only problem would be to determine if such a dire condition be shared by other, equally unfortunate, peoples. While ideas and passions can be substantial, peculiar, identity-bestowing factors, lack of them is not equally informative.

Shared values are, in themselves, an interesting problem: they seem to pre-exist law and politics, which are supposed to respect them, and on the other hand they sometimes look like the creation of law and politics.

13.2 Law ad Morality

We already find this problem in Dante's *Inferno*, when the reader runs into the very first properly damned soul with a name (after the Ignavi and Limbo, therefore in the Second Circle, where those who indulged in luxury eternally dwell and suffer)[3]:

"The first of those whose story you should know,"
my master wasted no time answering,
"was empress over lands of many tongues;

her vicious tastes had so corrupted her
she licensed every form of lust with laws
to cleanse the stain of scandal she had spread.

[2]Pasolini [1802] (1993).
[3]*Inf.*, V, 53–57.

She is Semiramis, who actually turned her libido, pleasure (*libito*) into licit (*licito*)—she decriminalized incest—in order not to be reproached, to cleanse the stain of scandal. This legal action seems to be graver than the scandalous conduct itself, even if it is just about words—in this case, the legal wording of the law.

The *crux* here is that while an evil action can have several ameliorating circumstances, because our flesh is so fragile, to claim and state that something evil is not that bad, to give an imprimatur to evil, is in itself one of the worst possible kinds of evil, because it alters the normative horizon where shared values dwell. The law wanted by Queen Semiramis (a Professor Braibanti on steroids) could nudge innocent souls into thinking that incest is not that bad after all, and that at the end of the day "love is love". This is exactly the theme touched by Gerolamo Cardano when he states that those who sin in public, those who praise the sin, seem to sin more gravely: it is a kind of public statement. It is a tampering with the narrative the shapes a normative horizon.[4]

The whole Quinta Cantica of Dante's *Inferno* could in fact be read as an attack against a specific kind of literature, the courtly romances, where adultery could be pictured as something glamorous and intriguing, thereby leading Paolo and Francesca da Rimini into an ill-starred forbidden love.[5] Laws against gay propaganda in Russia and Eastern Europe still follow this pattern of thought: it is not so much gay sex that is evil, but claiming that it is not (a claim implied in any open or "proud" out behavior).

Normative propositions can be performatively insidious, they can twist and cut the distance between *word* and *world*: a sinner can be absolved, but you cannot demand to sin with your bishop's blessing. The libertine politicians—Berlusconi or President Trump—can have their moral lapses, but they never officially claim that what they do is *licito*, is morally and *legally* ok (although they dog whistle that it is *fun*). They can repent and ask forgiveness (if they are Italian this usually happens, in old age after a life of decadent self-indulgence—something Pasolini would have not condoned). If however another kind of politician, supposedly chaste and disciplined, asks some kind of legal recognition for LGBTQIA couples, that is much worse, because this means messing with the shared normative horizon, changing the shared notion of what is *licito*.

The Catholic Church has a long history of interest in *words* and their power. The sacramental words *efficiunt quod figurant*, they carry out what they mean, they do turn the bread and the wine into the body and blood of Jesus Christ.[6]

A famous cardinal of the Catholic Church gave a famous formula for this normative phenomenon. His name was De Retz, and his *Memoirs*[7] were the last book read by Walter Benjamin before taking his own life. De Retz admired

[4]See in this volume, *Gerolamo Cardano and "Italian Realism"*, Sect. 4.2. Gerolamo Cardano, *Proxeneta, seu De Prudentia Civili*, Caput XXVII.

[5]Contini (1979).

[6]See in this volume, *The Limits of Law and Arturo Carlo Jemolo's Islands*, Sect. 11.1.

[7]de Gondi De Retz (1993), 2:60; 1:82.

Richelieu, but despised Mazarin (another cardinal), who eventually won the war between eminences; he belonged to the same family of Gilles De Rais (same pronunciation, not by chance), a sadist bisexual who, after horrific sexual crimes, repented and became a monk. De Retz is famous because David Hume quotes him in his *Treatise,* where it is said[8]

> that there are many things, in which the world wishes to be deceive d; and that it more easily excuses a person in acting than in talking contrary to the decorum of his profession and character.

Words can entail a graver offense than actions (this sounds truly like Cardano's *deterior est malo qui malum laudat, quod malus solus peccat*) because they interfere with those "many things", in which the world wishes to be deceived: i.e., the unreal and "false" stability and firmness of the normative horizon that co-exists with the jeopardized narrative. That normative horizon—any normative horizon—is neither stable nor firm, it is on the contrary fragile and vulnerable (as Braibanti's prosecutors vividly perceived), it does not rest on any "truth" (except the meta-truth according to which *falsis omnia debentur humana*) and even a film by an outraged movie director can be deemed as dangerous for it—as Pier Paolo Pasolini most famously learned at his own expenses.

Needless to say, Catholic cardinals are also aware that *legal* norms are especially dangerous. Joseph Ratzinger, as the Dean of the College of Cardinals, celebrated the mass *pro eligendo pontefice*, for the election of the Pope, just before secluding himself in the conclave that was going to elect him to the pontifical throne with the name of Benedict XVI. In his sermon, he also stated that law can affect morality. Mr. Eugenio Scalfari, founder of the most important left-leaning Italian newspaper, *la Repubblica*, found such a statement puzzling and bewildering—should not, for a Catholic, morality be able to change the law, rather than the other way around[9]? It was, of course, a fundamental misunderstanding. Law can impact that primary morality, that circle of shared values, those "many things, in which the world wishes to be deceived". Citizens and subjects, politicians and legislators can do this at their own peril. Those legal words could nudge the world into seeing as valuable actions, desires, lifestyles, behaviors that are actually and objectively sinful or disordered. This is hardly news: "law has also great symbolic and expressive value. Even when the decisions of legislatures and courts do not have very wide practical effect, they do make a statement".[10]

[8]Hume (1978), p. 153.

[9]Scalfari (2005), p. 1.

[10]Nussbaum (2008), p. 360.

13.3 Two Notions of Vulnerability, Again

The archbishop of the city where I live, Bologna, was Carlo Caffarra: he was one of the four (extremely conservative) bishops who raised their *dubia*, doubts, against the *Amoris Laetitia* wanted by Pope Francis. He was well known for his quite conservative positions. A learned scholar himself, he mentioned, in one of his papers, the Columbia legal philosopher Joseph Raz.

Caffarra warned that law, "shapes the public ethos and the beliefs of public reason". He then adds that, according to Raz, monogamy is not available to the individual per se: as an institution, monogamy needs some kind of public recognition and support. It is not that a single individual cannot reserve to a single partner all and any sexual intercourse, or that an individual cannot choose a traditional marriage. It is rather that marriage is a fragile, vulnerable institution if it is not supported, acknowledged, recognized, and the public reason orientation is a decisive factor in this supporting process. According to Caffarra, legally recognize gay unions (let alone same sex marriage) means to give up such a support—it is tantamount to tamper with the normative horizon that gives meaning to the institution of marriage.[11]

Here there are at stake two different notions of vulnerability. According to His Eminence, traditional marriage, our cherished institutions and traditions, our lifestyle, is fragile and vulnerable and should be protected by any attempt to tamper with it. Those institutions and traditions give shape and substance to "real" marriage, to the truth of marriage. It is some kind of anthropological, possibly metaphysically based, notion of vulnerability. Marriage is vulnerable the way saints can be, lofty and sublime figures always on the verge of being turned into martyrs.

From the point of view of the discriminated LGBTQIA people involved, there is a situated vulnerability contingently linked to their comprehensive group: meaningful rights, basically full citizenship rights, are denied together with what Vico would call "solemn nuptials".

As in the Braibanti case, we have here two kinds of vulnerabilities pitted one against the other. Now, however, some decades after Braibanti's imprisonment, the minority vulnerability has a name: it is not about a persecuted individual (gallantly defended by a handful of writers), but a minority comprehensive group with its peculiar identity. It is a situated vulnerability. It is about gay rights and marriage *equality*.

Since efficacy is essentially granular, point-like, punctual, although it can be perceived and construed as a stable and firm normative system, its ensuing narrative is specifically exposed to other efficacy phenomena, no matter how minimal to the subject's perception, by the very existence of such phenomena. A red dot is a red dot period, even if it is sided by a blue and a yellow dot. Once the blue and yellow dots are removed, and substituted with purple, scarlet, pink, and violet dots, the red dot has not changed a bit in itself—but that *in itself* does not exist as far as efficacy

[11] Caffarra (2006).

phenomena are concerned, because they are apprehended only through a non-neutral narrative. Therefore, while that red dot *was* actually one of the three primary colors, it is *now* the chromatic basis for a fan of color variations. It does not matter that the red has not changed a bit. Its "meaning" changed: the normative meaning of an efficacy phenomenon, apprehended through its narrative, is all that can be found in it. Behind the mask there is no face.

This means that Monsignor Caffarra was not completely wrong after all: from this point of view, marriage is no longer the same, when even gay and lesbians can wed. Once LGBTQIA people exist and are visible and legally recognized, they turn into a new unwelcome color dot—that changes the normative meaning of the (perceived) primary hue. There is a new narrative available. What His Eminence could not see, though, is that the very existence of an alternative narrative already implies a change: now the definition of traditional marriage must include a non-neutral will of not listening to such an alternative narrative.

13.4 Vulnerable Positions

Individuals like Braibanti, or members of minority encompassing groups, find themselves in a vulnerable position because they are deemed as at odds with the pre-existing mainstream narrative. In such mainstream narrative they can and must be sacrificed: compassion would imply a wound on itself, because behind the mainstream narrative itself there is no harder, more fundamental, reality.

In order to shed light on this fascinating point, I shall make use of the verses from the immortal *Orlando in Love* by Matteo Maria Boiardo. The scene is a usual one: Orlando is fighting an Orc, and the evil creature, before definitely succumbing, manages to activate a secret trap, an iron net that captures the paladin—who is therefore helplessly hanging down from a tree. Orlando is almost invulnerable, but he could well die of starvation; luckily, however, someone is approaching on the road: a friar. The Count is quick in asking for help, but the friar (who also found Orlando's sword quite heavy, and difficult to use), has a different point of view.[12]

[12]Boiardo [1495] (1995), Vol. I, pp. 17–20.

Diceva il conte: pigliate il mio brando,
E sopra a me questa rete tagliate. -
Rispose il frate: A Dio te racomando,
S'io te occidessi, io seria irregulare;
Questa malvagità non voglio fare.
Vogli morir dicea come cristiano,
Né ti voler per questo disperare.
Abbi speranza nel Segnor soprano,
Che, avendo in pacienza questa morte,
Te farà cavallier della sua corte.
[…]
Molte altre cose assai gli sapea dire,
E tutto il martilogio gli ha contato,
La pena che ogni Santo ebbe a soffrire:
Chi crucifisso, e chi fo scorticato.
Dicea: -Figliolo, il te convien morire:
Abbine Dio del celo ringraziato. –

Said The Count: "Take my sword,
Cut this net in which I am in".
Said the friar: "God's my Lord,
If I killed you, it'd be grave sin.
With such evil I can't cope:
Like a Christian you should die,
Neither you should lose your hope.
In the Lord just put your sight
For accepting death and pain,
He will knight you in his Reign.
[…]
Many tales the friar told
Of the martyr saints who died
and much pain sustained of old:
skinned alive and crucified.
"You must die", the friar said,
Just be grateful, don't be mad.

Orlando's reply is interesting[13]:

[13] Boiardo (1995), Vol. I, pp. 20–21.

Rispose Orlando, con parlar modesto:
Ringraziato sia lui, ma non di questo.
[…]
Perch'io vorrebbi aiuto, e non conforto.
Mal aggia l'asinel che t'ha portato!
Se un giovane venia, non seria morto.

Orlando then with modesty replied
I thank him sure –not for such aid.
[…]
Because I do need help, and no comfort
Be cursed the ass that brought you here,
A young man would've spared me such a tort.

Orlando finds himself in a painful, dangerous position. The cowardly friar is nevertheless not interest in his position, but only in his own—if he killed Orlando *his* soul would be in peril. The Count's peculiar existential position does not matter, and the informed consent given by Orlando (the friar is not aware that Orlando is invulnerable) does not either. The friar does not believe that Orlando can be the best judge of what he needs, and he offers instead palliative comfort, the inspiring tales of Christian martyrs. He seems to see Orlando's pain and death as something valuable from an objective point of view: his soul will be saved, he will be a knight in the Heavenly Court.

The friar acts on a rationale that is external to Orlando's situation: there are rules that are not only valid always, *semper*, but also in all possible circumstances, *ad semper*. Acting against life, conceived as a fundamental aspect of human flourishing, is always forbidden—there are things that are *intrinsece mala*, evil in themselves.[14] The cry of those who find themselves in a vulnerable position, caught in a normative net that jeopardizes their existence (as situated members of that encompassing group), cannot be listened to.

Eluana Englaro was a young woman who had already lived for many years a mere vegetative life; her father, Beppino, who knew what would have been Eluana's choice (something confirmed by many witnesses), tried hard to have the hydration system removed that alone would keep her "alive". Both Eluana and Beppino were caught in the law's iron net: they could not be helped, because to detach Eluana's body from that machinery would have been an act against life, murder. Eluana and Beppino's cry could not be listened to: and therefore, Eluana was forbidden to be herself, a young woman who would have loathed the idea of surviving her own death. Beppino finally found a legal way to free her daughter, and took her to the clinic where they were going to follow a protocol. Eluana's heart was supposed to stop in some days. The Berlusconi administration managed to enact a new law to stop the procedure. Eluana's system, however, shut down ahead of time, depriving

[14] Mitchell Finnis (1991).

her torturers of the last minute victory show: embittered and frustrated, they whispered of poison.

Situated vulnerability is always normative vulnerability; a given instance of vulnerability is addressed by carrying out an equality practice. The trouble is, an equality practice is not necessarily an intellectual, scholarly contribution: it can be a political fight, and one that does not need to be smooth and nice. Sometimes those who carry out such practices are and stay unsung heroes, because they simply give a contribution to the creation of an alternative narrative, drops of paint of a different color that seamlessly coagulate in a strange new chromatic dot. They do not need to look like consistent characters, or soldiers of the same army.

Sometimes circumstances allow a few of them to get an unwanted notoriety—this is what happened to Beppino Englaro. The outrageous life, and cruel death, of Pier Paolo Pasolini was just another of those normative drops, liable to nudge, in a direction he would have probably not really liked or endorsed, toward a new narrative. His poem was a performative contradiction: by desperately crying that all Italian feelings are not real, not authentic, he managed to produce a lasting one.

References

Boiardo M-M [1483] (1995) Orlando Innamorato. In: Bruscagli R (ed) Orlando Innamorato. Einaudi, Turin

Caffarra C (2006) Matrimonio e laicità dello Stato. Opening Session of the International Teologico-Pastoral Conference in Valencia, Spain, 4 July

Contini G (1979) Un'idea di Dante. Saggi danteschi. Einaudi, Turin

Cuoco V (2014) Historical Essay on the Neapolitan Revolution of 1799. In: Haddock B, Sabetti F (eds) (trans: Gibbons D). University Press Toronto, Toronto

de Gondi De Retz (1993) Memoirs. Gallimard, Paris

Hume D [1740] (1978) A treatise of human nature. Clarendon, Oxford

Mitchell Finnis J (1991) Moral absolutes. Tradition, revision, and truth. The Catholic University of America Press, Washington

Nussbaum M (2008) Liberty of conscience. In: Defence of America's tradition of religious equality. Basic Books, New York

Pasolini P-P [1964] La Guinea. In: Pasolini P-P (1993) Poesia in forma di rosa. Garzanti, Milano

Scalfari E (2005) Missionario nell'Europa miscredente. La Repubblica. April 21:1

Viglione M (2016) Il problema della legittimità della Rivoluzione Francese in Vincenzo Cuoco. Il dibattito storiografico e riflessioni aggiuntive. "RiMe". Rivista dell'Istituto di Storia dell'Europa Mediterranea 16(2):197–226

MIX
Papier aus verantwortungsvollen Quellen
Paper from responsible sources
FSC® C105338

If you have any concerns about our products,
you can contact us on
ProductSafety@springernature.com

In case Publisher is established outside the EU,
the EU authorized representative is:
Springer Nature Customer Service Center GmbH
Europaplatz 3, 69115 Heidelberg, Germany

Printed by Libri Plureos GmbH
in Hamburg, Germany